THE BEST OF
Only in L.A.

In the 1930s, the L.A. Chamber of Commerce sent gag photos like this to East Coast newspapers in hopes of drumming up tourist interest.

THE BEST OF

Only in L.A.

a chronicle of
the amazing, amusing and absurd

by los angeles times columnist
steve harvey

LOS ANGELES TIMES   TIMES MIRROR SQUARE   LOS ANGELES, CALIFORNIA

Guide to cover photos:

Street sign	Page 57
Clown	Page 218
Student driver	Page 74
Man and sculpture	Page 210

Los Angeles Times

Publisher: Richard T. Schlosberg III
Editor: Shelby Coffey III

Los Angeles Times Syndicate

President and CEO: Jesse Levine
VP/General Manager, Domestic: Steve Christensen

Director of Book Development: Don Michel
Book Editor: Noel Greenwood
Book Designer: Patricia Moritz

Library of Congress Catalogue Number: 96-076767
ISBN 1-883792-12-6
Copyright © 1996, Los Angeles Times

Published by the Los Angeles Times Syndicate
Times Mirror Square, Los Angeles, California 90053
A Times Mirror Company

First printing, May 1996

Printed in the U.S.A.

foreword

    Steve Harvey regularly works his sly magic on the people and places in that state of mind known as L.A. His column is filled with wry takes on the city that gave us disasters of legend like the "Day of the Locust" and disasters of reality like the Northridge earthquake of 1994. Not to mention the delights of Marilyn Monroe films, West Coast rap, the Getty Museum, Laker Magic and California dreaming, both vintage and new.

    Steve lures readers with oddities and amusements that bubble up here like strange brew from the fabled La Brea Tar Pits...The thieves who made off with several bags of designer shoes, not realizing they were all for the left foot...The Burbank resident who left a warning sign at his house, "Pit Bull on Angel Dust"...The "Don't Walk" signal that showed an electronic hand with only the middle finger extended—now that's a stop sign. Steve finds them all, polishes the tales and presents them in his daily jewel box.

    Over the years, thousands of readers have added to the jewel box, writing to Steve to tell of their sightings and experiences. For a paper like the Los Angeles Times, which has 3 million readers a day spread out over Southern California, Steve serves as a contact point, a center of sanity in a world often delightfully mad, and sometimes just plain zany—but in the L.A. way.

    His column has helped to define that attitude of watchful amusement that is essential to living in Los Angeles: a bit cool, a bit detached. It's the attitude that allows you to be momentarily fascinated by a famous face on a Beverly Hills street corner—but to simultaneously wonder if it belongs to one of those impersonators who advertise in the paper as look-alikes for office parties. And is that fellow lying down just behind the famous face blissed-out, or taking a nap, or just plain dead?

    Steve Harvey's "Best of Only in L.A." will prepare you for moments like these. Read on.

Shelby Coffey III
Editor, Los Angeles Times

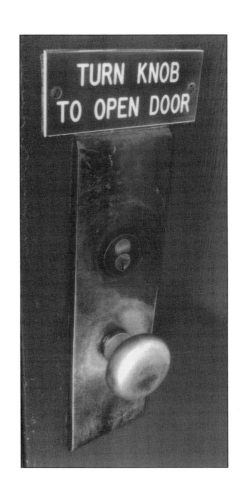

introduction

At every newspaper, there's one reporter who gets the assignment when an eccentric character appears in the lobby with a build-it-yourself coffin kit or soap sculptures of the Presidents or a song celebrating Culver City.

At the L.A. Times, I was that reporter.

My usual routine was to listen to the visitor's story and then send him on his way with a small fib like, "You know, we already have several songs about Culver City. Now if you could write one about Lawndale…"

Then, one day in 1988, I was assigned to write the "Only in L.A." column. Suddenly, I saw the lobby visitors in a different light. They could provide me with material that would fit perfectly in a column about the wacky side of L.A.

•

The column quickly developed its own personality. Items ran the gamut from celebrity madams and nude pen-pal clubs to a doomsdayer with antennae in his ears, a brassiere museum and a voter who registered as God. I also plucked material from the daily flow of news events: the City Council follies, oddball crimes, unusual lawsuits, and so on. I supplemented this with my lobby visitors, including one gentleman with a collection of 10,000 autographs (few scrawled by anyone famous — he just asked everyone he met for their signatures).

Readers began sending me material, and I printed the names of contributors whose items I used. That sent the column in a different direction. It became a sort of daffy dialogue with readers. Soon I was receiving photos of signs that made no sense, advertisements with misspellings that changed their meaning, and menus with laughable errors. Some topics inspired the creation of regular departments within the column, like "Dueling Signs" and "Stupid Criminal Tricks."

I also sensed the column had become a sounding board for people upset (or bemused) at being treated like numbers. Readers mailed in parking tickets sent to people who had died months before, computer-generated letters that seemed to be written in another language (one, in fact, was), and DWP bills for outrageous (and erroneous) amounts. When the IRS issued a memo admitting that one of its forms contained an error, a reader asked me: "How come the IRS can fine us for mistakes, but we can't fine them?" Well, we may not be able to fine the IRS, but we can needle them a little bit in "Only in L.A."

Still, humor remained the overriding theme—like the computerized contest letter that promised one reader, "You'll be turning quite a few heads on the streets of Los Angeles as you roar down P.O. Box 3543 in your new Corvette."

Readers also sent along countless personal anecdotes, some easier to verify than others. I never did print one person's sighting of a topless go-go dancer, said to be standing in the back of a pick-up truck on the freeway, holding a Bill Clinton-for-President sign during the 1992 campaign. (Sure, it sounded plausible, but...)

Nor did I fall for the guy who claimed to be a Culver City cop. He said he had ticketed a mortician for driving in a car pool lane on the San Diego Freeway. The mortician's supposed excuse was that the corpse was her passenger. However, the cop's name didn't check out with the police department. So I did the next best thing—I ran an item about the hoax attempt.

Careful as I tried to be, I made my share of mistakes—which many readers delighted in pointing out. Some pet lovers have never forgiven me for confusing a cockatoo and a cockatiel (one's a dog and one's a bird, but don't ask me which). Another error, referring to a kangaroo with a pouch as a "he," was just as egregious, but drew fewer letters. Thankfully, there aren't that many kangaroo owners out there.

Some items that readers submitted were a bit too risque for a family newspaper (you'd be surprised how often "public" turns up spelled as "pubic"). While such items didn't make it into my column, some of them are in this book.

•

Over the years, the letters and phone calls have increased (I now receive about 100 per week of each) and the column has attracted even wider attention. Maybe "notoriety" would be a better way to put it. I remember the pride I felt when a press aide for a City Council member recognized my name. I had phoned about his boss's public demonstration of a new low-flush toilet. The aide said, "No offense, Steve, but we were hoping the Times would do a real story on this."

Regular readers know that although the column is entitled "Only in L.A.," much of the material is about people or events outside the city itself. That's because I've always thought of "L.A." more as a frame of mind, an expression of whatever it is that connects the people who live in this region.

Even with this expansive view of L.A., there are days when getting good material for the column is a real challenge. I find myself a couple of hours away from deadline with nothing more than a misspelled reference to "potatoe" (accompanied by a Dan Quayle joke, of course) and a screenwriter's plea for a plug.

Then there are times when terrific items seem to materialize out of nowhere. I'll never forget the day a man jumped off the Santa Monica Pier and was saved because help was summoned by three passersby—Heidi Fleiss, a TV newsman and Michael Jackson's plastic surgeon.

Clearly, this was an event made for "Only in L.A." You can imagine how excited I was. Until an editor told me, "Sorry, Steve, but we're going to do a real story on it."

Luckily, with the help of readers, I've managed to gather (and hang on to) plenty of other intriguing items over the past eight years. Enough to fill a real book, in fact. Who needs Heidi anyway?

contents

people 12
The Playboy model who used her centerfold as an I.D...The ocean-going wallet that finally returned home...Mr. R. U. Kidding? and other memorable names...The $100 priestess...Skid Row's most unsentimental hotel clerk.

lifestyles 20
Getting by in upscale L.A...The definitely unofficial Barbie diaries...A freeway marriage proposal and other romantic impulses...More L.A. bashing...Our intimate habits exposed (almost half of us start the day before 6 a.m.).

history 42
Translating from the Spanish (welcome to Executioner Hills)...Celebrity landmarks, including intersections...Our age-old debate over how to say El Lay...The famed gunslinger who became (what else?) a technical adviser to filmmakers.

disasters 58
Earthquake: A list that may cause you to lose some sleep...Riot: the priest and Ava Gardner's pantaloons...Fire: some of the dumbest 911 calls...Drought: if there's no water for grass, green gravel will do just fine.

driving 68
God is a licensed driver, and other tales of the DMV...Vanity plates that spelled trouble...World's toughest meter maids...Bulletins from the parking wars...The errant golf ball and other freeway tales...How we used to drive.

the law 92
The steamroller as getaway car, and other stupid criminal tricks...The case of the giant foam rubber breasts...Stories from the not-exactly-a-crime file...When lawyers upset judges (or, you'll never single-space in this town again).

politics 114
L.A. and the Presidency (learn which former President once sold drill bits here)...The dead candidate who won the election anyhow...Sonny Bono articulates on articulation...Notes from the campaign trail...Our Watergate grads.

government 120
The DWP's better ideas (like bottled water for its offices)...Flying chairs, fistfights and other civic disturbances...Irwindale's Hungarian flag salute to Mexican independence...Keeping our school children safe from the dreaded backward R.

media 130
Hello, this is the AP tree...Memorable (and not so memorable) TV news slogans...A disc jockey's exploding toilet hoax...An obituary for Victor Frisbie, who never really existed...The blooper file.

x

Not a neighbor to trifle with.

people

The Playboy model who used her **centerfold as an I.D**...

The ocean-going wallet that finally returned home...

Mr. R. U. Kidding? and other memorable names...**The $100 priestess**...Skid Row's most unsentimental hotel clerk.

After a young woman wrote a check at a clothes store in Marina del Rey, the clerk asked to see her driver's license. She explained apologetically that her wallet had been stolen. But, she added, she did have one form of ID.

"I was the May centerfold in Playboy magaine," she said. "I have the centerfold here in my purse if you want to see it."

She took it out. The smiles matched.

▼

A woman loitering at a garage sale in Pacific Palisades was observed covertly affixing a flyer to one of the tables. The flyer advertised her own garage sale a few blocks away.

▼

A young lady with "sort of a Russian accent" filled out an application for a waitressing job at a Hollywood cafe. After she left, bartender Chris Ausbon scanned the form. All seemed in order until Ausbon got to the box marked "sex." Instead of the standard "male" or "female" response, the young woman had written: "Virgin."

▼

As the checker at a Brentwood supermarket finished with a customer, she chirped: "Have a nice day."

"No thanks, I have other plans," he growled. "But you go ahead."

*And bring your driver's
license for identification.*

A Catalina checklist: Among the odd questions that would-be visitors ask when they phone the Catalina Island Chamber of Commerce:

  "Do I need a passport?"

  "What type of currency do you use?"

  "Is there water on the other side of the island?"

  "Is it true that you don't have to pay taxes?"

  "How far from the beach is the water."

When Nissen Davis of Rancho Palos Verdes ran a classified ad for an *au pair* to assist with child care, he received a call from a retiree who wanted the job for himself and his wife. Informed that the Davises were seeking a young foreign student, the caller asked: "Then why advertise for an old pair?"

▼

Generation gap: A youthful clerk in a San Gabriel music store was asked if she could find a copy of Handel's "Messiah."

The clerk punched an inquiry into her computer, then said: "The only thing we have by that group is a single." What "group" did she mean? The rock group Messiah, she responded.

▼

A Sherman Oaks resident observed a passerby inspecting a set of Venetian blinds that she had put out with the trash. "We're throwing those away," the resident said. "You can have them if you want."

"I don't know," the passerby said. "I'm not crazy about the color."

▼

A Glendale man found the restroom lines so long during an Eagles concert at Irvine Meadows that he crept over to a secluded area to answer the call of nature. When he turned around he saw, to his surprise, more than a dozen other men waiting in an orderly line behind him.

▼

Dick Sheets of Granada Hills had to know why the downtown street evangelist stood there with a plastic cup on his head. "So one day I asked him," Sheets related. "He told me that the cup had water in it. He used to leave it on the curb, but people walking by would drop cigarette butts in it or spit in it or leaves would fall in it. So he just put it on his head. He didn't think it was too unusual."

small world dept.

Vincent Rogers was intrigued when his son, Michael, a Hollywood musician, purchased a 1948 Packard. The elder Rogers had once owned the same model himself. He reminisced about his old car, and mentioned doing some repair work on the right fender. Surprisingly, the fender on the son's Packard showed evidence of the same repairs. Then Vincent checked his records and found that the engine number on his old Packard matched that of Michael's. It was the same car, back in the family nearly 40 years later.

▼

Sheriff's Deputy Louis Lotgering, answering a burglary call, couldn't help noticing the blue customized Datsun pickup parked in the driveway. The reason: it was his truck, stolen three years earlier from his home in Burbank. A Temple City man who said he had "borrowed" the truck from a friend was taken into custody.

▼

Lois Queener long ago had lost her gold-plated bracelet, the one engraved with the date of her graduation from a Kansas high school. Now she was a saleswoman at Sherman Oaks Antique Mall. One day, a jewelry dealer stopped by to show some pieces that he wanted to sell. Queener looked closely at one, then declared: "This is my bracelet." Sure enough, the engraved date was still there, along with her name. The dealer had found the bracelet in a thrift shop in Wisconsin. Queener's boss bought it for her on the spot.

▼

Writer Karen Stabiner lost her wallet during a cloudburst in Santa Monica. Five days later, a lifeguard returned it to her. The wallet had been found on the beach, apparently after making its way into a storm drain, floating out to the ocean, and then washing ashore. It still contained her driver's license and credit cards — and her yogurt bonus card.

An X-rated yard sale.

Who is that strange man in my lettuce? At a Fourth of July show at Pierce College, a parachutist attemping to land on the stadium field instead plopped down on a salad table set up for VIPs. No one was injured.

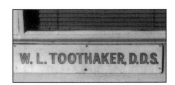

memorable names

Denis O'Pray, rector of the Church of Our Saviour in San Gabriel.

Jesse James, **Harry Hollywood** and **Sherman Oaks**, LAPD officers.

Daniel Waters and Norman Powers, officials in the Department of Water and Power.

Jim Crooks, chief of L.A. County criminal justice computer system.

George Crook, an L.A. lawyer. After he won a Golden Moniker Award from California Lawyer magazine, he wrote to the publication, "I am not a Nixon."

John Argue, L.A. lawyer.

Susan Tellem, public relations executive.

Norm Reeder, in charge of Torrance library programs.

Jay Carsman, coordinator of L.A. city parking systems.

Vincent Moneymaker and Richard Moneymaker, L.A. bankruptcy attorneys.

Steve Bear, an Angeles National Forest ranger.

Michael Park, a city Recreation and Parks supervisor.

Mark Ussery, loan department employee at Western Federal Savings and Loan.

you can go home again— with certain restrictions

Above it all: Larry Walters' memorable flight took him only from San Pedro to Long Beach, but he did it in a lawn chair suspended from weather balloons. "It was a lifelong dream," he told reporters. Walters, who landed by deflating the balloons with a pellet gun, encountered only one obstacle: the Federal Aviation Administration, which fined him $1,500.

A Los Angeles man lived as a child in a downtown hotel owned by his family. Thirty years later, he paid a nostalgic visit to the hotel, long since sold by his family and surrounded now by Skid Row.

He approached the desk clerk, told his story, and asked if he could look around inside. After all, the place held so many memories for him.

"You got a room key?" the clerk asked.

"No," he said.

"Get the hell out of here," the clerk said.

just clowning around

Police were a bit taken aback when they arrived at the West L.A. residence of one R.U. Kidding? and were told that a violin, costumes and makeup had been stolen. "I'm a professional clown," explained the victim, who had legally changed his name from Joseph Copeland to R.U. Kidding?—question mark included.

she redefined 'sacrifice'

Self-described high priestess Mary Ellen Tracy, convicted of prostitution charges, claimed that she was merely holding religious services. The Silver Lake woman said one of her church's rituals called for male "worshipers" to have sex with her in exchange for monetary "sacrifices" in excess of $100.

it's about time...

Ramon Arnaga finally took care of the $11.37 bill he had owed the L.A. Times for 23 years. Arnaga, a retired maitre d' and voice coach in Hollywood, had left the bill in a suitcase that he loaned to a nephew in 1967. The nephew moved to France and Arnaga forgot about the bill. When the nephew returned the suitcase in 1990, the bill was still there. Arnaga sent the Times a check for $27, adding: "I hope that takes care of the interest."

food for thought

Advertising writer Craig Copeland, after being laid off by a Beverly Hills agency, stood at a streetcorner with a sign that said: "Will write ad copy for food." The offer was not completely in jest. Copeland said that "to get my foot into the door, to show someone what I can do, I would work for food." Passersby seemed sympathetic but confused, he said.

Signs like this were a hit among L.A. panhandlers, who displayed them on street corners from Malibu to Covina. They became so familiar that a Pasadena store spoofed them in a holiday display: a homeless Santa mannequin pushing a shopping cart with a sign reading, "Why Lie? I Need an Egg Nog."

A tourist entering the ritzy Paseo Nuevo shopping center in Santa Barbara heard this demand from a panhandler: "Spare change so I can buy a condo in L.A.?"

A gentleman in a three-piece suit needed change for an extra six minutes on his parking meter on Santa Monica Boulevard. So he did the logical thing. He bummed a dime off a street person standing nearby.

A visitor from New York was approached on Hollywood Boulevard by a panhandler who asked: "Would you like to buy some gravel from Michael Jackson's driveway?"

A street person carrying a gasoline can walked up to a shopper at a Culver City mall and said: "I ran out of gas. Can you give me some money?" It was the identical routine the panhandler had used with the same shopper a few weeks earlier.

"Your car sure runs out of gas a lot," said the shopper. "You ought to get your fuel gauge fixed."

"Oh," the panhandler quickly replied, "that was my other car."

TRICKS OF THE TRADE: A downtown panhandler who had the unmistakable look of pregnancy said she needed money for food. So a sympathetic passerby gave her $3. Later that day, the passerby saw the same panhandler again, but this time she did not appear pregnant. In fact, she looked slim. "Must have been a pretty easy delivery," the passerby said. The panhandler just winked.

Bill Cohen of West Covina pulled into a gas station and encountered a panhandler talking into a portable phone. Said an amazed Cohen: "He stopped the conversation to ask for some spare change, I said no, and he went back to his conversation and walked away."

Ed Stalcup of Malibu was walking through a parking lot near the beach when a panhandler asked him: "Say, man, do you have any extra change? I want to get an avocado and watercress sandwich."

A beach-goer on an early morning walk in Malibu with his dog heard a beeper go off. Upon investigation, he discovered a battery-operated motion detector — installed by a transient camped in some nearby rocks.

The widow of singer Roger Miller, who wrote and sang "King of the Road," donated 14 boxes of his clothing and shoes to the National Hobo Assn. The duds were passed out at a hobo tribute to Miller in Colton, where the Santa Fe, Southern Pacific and Union Pacific railroads intersected.

On Melrose Avenue, a young man held a cardboard sign that asked for "spare change so I can get my nose pierced."

A panhandler with a wry sense of humor displayed this sign at an outdoor mall in Santa Monica: "A Bum Holding a Sign."

On Sunset Boulevard, a man in a white robe held up a sign that said: "Will give karate training for food."

Bumper sticker on an old VW van: "Will Be President for Food."

Motorists plunking coins into the cup of a panhandler at a traffic light seemed to be responding to his understated approach. His sign said: "One penny, please."

Panhandler's sign lets you know he is on his lunch break.

On a Santa Monica Freeway off-ramp, a young man held a sign reading: "Need Money for Organically Grown Vegetarian Raw Food."

people

With dietary advice like this, a lot of shoppers thought a new health food store had opened. It turned out to be a Chinese supermarket in Monterey Park with a name that loosely translates as "prosperous."

lifestyles

Getting by in **upscale L.A**....The definitely unofficial **Barbie diaries**...A **freeway marriage proposal** and other romantic impulses...**More L.A. bashing**...Our intimate **habits** exposed (almost half of us start the day before 6 a.m.).

Twenty-five portraits of dachshunds by artist David Hockney hung on the walls of a gallery in Venice. A visitor, pleased that her male companion seemed to be showing interest in the art, confided to another spectator: "I've never taken him to an art gallery before, but he just had to see this show." Yes, her male companion was a dachshund.

▼

Even in these tense times, you can still find traces of Southern California's lazy charm. Such as the Culver City bus with its electronic destination sign that read: "Nowhere Particular."

▼

Poppy Cleaners displayed a sign reading: "Wedding Gowns and Leather." Well, Poppy *is* located in West Hollywood.

▼

A Torrance company was the co-developer of a motor-driven water bed that could move from room to room at a top speed of 3 m.p.h.

▼

As the Rolling Stones performed on the stage of the Rose Bowl, a spectator called a friend on her portable phone, then pointed the phone toward the stage. "He's a big Stones fan, but he couldn't make it to the concert," she explained to a seat-mate.

miscelLAny

Gay and lesbian vegetarians with a sense of humor formed a cooking group called Passion Fruits.

The most popular names for boys born during a 12-month period in L.A. County: Jose, Michael, Daniel, David and Christopher, in that order. For girls: Jessica, Stephanie, Jennifer, Maria and Elizabeth.

The magazine USC Business estimated that graduates of the university's business school own 12,240 Oriental rugs.

A transvestite group based in Woodland Hills called itself The Valley Girls and circulated a monthly newsletter entitled "Cross-Talk." A spokesman for the all-male membership explained: "We want to reach out to cross-dressers who are scared to death that what they're doing is wrong and that they are the only ones who do it."

▼

When someone posted a for-sale notice for a fur coat on the bulletin board of a Manhattan Beach health club, it started a small graffiti war. "It's dead," someone wrote across the notice. Then came this scrawled response: "So are your shoes and dinner."

▼

Seen on a South Bay road: a motorcyclist on a salmon pink chopper, wearing a black leather jacket with this legend on the back: "Hell's Yuppies, Palos Verdes, Calif."

where all the flowers have gone

Descanso Gardens in La Canada Flintridge has the world's largest collection of camellias (over 100,000 plants of 600 species), according to the book "The City Observed."

Glendora is believed to have the nation's largest growth of bougainvillea, a plant first brought there on whaling ships in the 1880s. The scarlet vines have been measured at a height of about 70 feet.

Pomona claims to have introduced to the United States that creeping vegetation known as Bermuda or Devil's grass.

Echo Park northwest of the Civic Center has one of the nation's largest growths of Oriental lotuses. They are said to have been the gift of evangelist Aimee Semple McPherson, who preached at the nearby Angelus Temple earlier this century.

more l.a. bashing

Two from the flake file: (1) After snow fell in parts of L.A. County one winter, the Philadelphia Daily News headlined its weather story this way: "L.A. Sees Another Kind of Flake." (2) A ski resort sign on U.S. 395 near Lone Pine contended: "We have more flakes than Venice Beach."

▼

A cartoon in the New Yorker depicted a man talking to his wife while watering the lawn. "You know what I like about L.A.?" he says. "We don't have to be interesting anymore."

▼

Bumper sticker in San Luis Obispo: "Conserve Water—Move to L.A."

▼

Johnny Carson said it: "On a daily average, Burbank airport has 94 departures. No arrivals, just departures."

▼

A woman newly arrived from Southern California placed a personal ad in the Seattle Weekly, hoping to meet fellow Californians. Instead, reported Lear's magazine, "She was besieged by calls from angry Seattle natives telling her in no uncertain terms to go back where she came from."

▼

Herb Caen, the San Francisco columnist, noted this headline in a Stockton newspaper: "Crooked Cop Gets 5 Years in L.A." Said Caen, "That'll show the mizzerable creep."

Postcard insult from our neighbors in Nevada.

The Perils of Peacekeeping: Bosnia, Los Angeles, Rwanda, Somalia…
10:00 a.m. – 11:30 a.m., Wednesday, January 18

At least L.A. hasn't required a U.N. force: Excerpt from program at a San Diego seminar.

the barbie diaries

Here are some entries you won't find in the official diary of Barbie, the ubiquitous doll that is a product of El Segundo toymaker Mattel:

May, 1990 – A couple billed as Barbie and Malibu Ken are sued by Mattel after they perform a striptease on television's "Donahue" show.

October, 1992 – The National Council of Teachers of Mathematics gives Mattel a failing grade for a Teen Talk Barbie Doll that says: "Math class is tough."

Joanna Linkchorst of Montrose found these G-rated instructions on a T-shirt: "Machine wash and tumble dry your silk screen T-shirt, clean your room and don't stay out past 11 without calling."

April, 1993 – The book "Mondo Barbie" offers a collection of stories with such characters as Hell's Angel Barbie, Twelve-Step Barbie and Van Nuys Barbie. Twelve-Step Barbie's girlfriend is Kendra, who was Ken before undergoing a sex-change operation.

July, 1993 – A Bay Area woman is ordered to shut down a Barbie Channeling Newsletter that dispenses saucy advice. Sample reader question: "Is there a bad Barbie?" The newsletter's answer: "The only bad Barbie is a bored Barbie."

December, 1993 – A group calling itself the Barbie Liberation Organization switches the voice boxes of some Barbie and G.I. Joe dolls in San Diego and other cities. The new Barbie growls: "Dead men tell no lies," while G.I. Joe chirps, "Want to go shopping?"

The welcome mat of the 90s.

24

upscale l.a.

After the Northridge earthquake, nervous residents could be seen stocking up on supplies all over the Southland. But Westsiders still had standards to observe. A woman appeared at a convenience store on Montana Avenue in Santa Monica and breathlessly asked:

"Sir, I need bread. Do you have any bread?"

"I only have day-old bread," replied the proprietor, whose store was a shambles.

The woman hesitated. "Oh," she said. "Wait just a minute. I'll have to check with my husband."

She scurried out to a nearby parking lot to consult, then returned and announced: "He says if that's all you've got, we'll take it."

▼

Remember when schools raised money with car washes? They did it differently one year at Franklin Elementary School on trendy Montana Avenue in Santa Monica. The donated items in a silent auction included a consultation with a fertility specialist, walk-on parts in two TV shows and a seven-day Caribbean cruise for two.

▼

The announcement from an eatery in a posh neighborhood declared: "It's finally here after three years in the making! We can now offer espresso, cappuccino, latte, mocha, specialty coffees." But who would expect anything less from McDonald's of Rolling Hills?

▼

In a story in Alaska Airlines magazine, the general manager of the posh Hotel Bel-Air was asked why residents from million-dollar estates in the neighborhood occasionally checked into the hotel. "Sometimes, they just don't want to deal with the mess in their houses," he explained.

miscelLAny

The color scheme of the Beverly Center mall at Beverly and La Cienega boulevards was changed from blue to brown, reportedly because retail experts believed that women were less inclined to shop in a blue building.

A "defecation bag" flown on an American shuttle mission—but never used—sold for $350 at a Beverly Hills auction of space memorabilia.

Where bad hair days are a real crisis: After taking up residence in affluent San Marino, Lori Levi received a welcome note from a dentist as well as a sticker on which emergency numbers could be written. There were spaces for Physician, Veterinarian — and Hair Salon.

▼

The sign taped to the utility pole read: "Desperate upper-middle-class Encino family garage sale. Need money. It was either sell the sailboat and airplane or else these wonderful items."

▼

Notice at a fund-raising auction for the Leo Baeck Temple on the Westside: "Dr. Steven Dresner, a well-known and respected ophthalmic plastic surgeon, has very generously donated an upper or lower eyelid cosmetic surgery…Value: $2,500." There was a slight catch, however: "Anesthesia fees are not included."

▼

The percentage of affluent Angelenos who say they couldn't do without: microwave ovens (60%), answering machines (53%), home computers (47%), maids or housekeepers (28%), deluxe hotel reservations when traveling (20%), car phones (15%), health club memberships (15%) and swimming pools (8%).

> PICK UP
> 1) cassette
> 2) exercise Book
> 3) Make Protein drink
> 4) clean gun

Found on an L.A. street: a typical Angeleno's list of things to do?

you know you're in beverly hills when:

You phone the police department, you're put on hold, and classical music plays.

▼

A water bar opens with 51 chilled varieties at $1 to $2 a glass, ice not included because it would "void out the subtleties."

▼

A specialty store stocks several models of gas-powered, miniature cars for children, including a 6-foot-long mini-Jaguar ($3,495) and a 9-foot-long Ferrari Testarossa ($15,000).

▼

More licenses are issued for gardening than any other business.

▼

The trendy store Camp Beverly Hills stages a Thanksgiving food drive for the homeless and finds the following items among the donations: sauerkraut, pickles, jalapeno jelly and sliced button mushrooms.

▼

A children's clothing store posts this sign: "Free Gianni Versace T-Shirt With Every $500 Purchase."

▼

The post office offers valet parking.

▼

Parking tickets are put inside protective coverings on rainy days.

Exhibits at an ecological exposition: shoes made from recycled tires and diapers, a dress consisting of 500 bottle caps and carpeting made from recycled soda bottles.

What clean-up crews found in L.A.'s canyons and beaches: a fake $20 bill, a plastic Santa Claus and sleigh, a fishing line with worms attached to stockings, a prosthetic joint, a giant Ronald McDonald doll, a 4-foot-high bottle of Scotch on a pedestal, blown-up safes, a Pepsi machine, a hot tub sawed in half and a telephone booth (with telephone).

please, no cash

Irene Machuca of Manhattan Beach pulled out two $20 bills and some change for a purchase at a Pac Tel Cellular office. The panicky clerk asked: "Don't you have a check or credit card? We aren't set up to handle cash."

▼

Marty Girvan of Pasadena witnessed this scene in a grocery store: "The person in front of me was paying cash, and the clerk, before accepting his money, asked him if he had any identification."

▼

L.A. school teacher Darci Knight wrote a $60 check to pay the fee for a special credential. "We don't take checks anymore," a school district clerk told her.

"I'll just pay in cash then," said the teacher.

"We don't take that, either. We only take postal money orders," the clerk replied.

"What do you mean?" asked an incredulous Knight.

Replied the clerk: "The person that used to handle the cash and checks got laid off."

the mean sidewalks of l.a.

In a ranking of 36 big cities according to their respect for pedestrians, L.A. finished a disappointing 34th.

Five experiments were conducted to see how downtown passersby would react to pedestrians who needed help. One researcher posing as a pedestrian with a leg brace spilled a load of magazines. "People looked at me but just didn't seem to want to bother," said the researcher. "One man walked very close to me, checked out the situation and then sidestepped around without a word."

Only New York City and Paterson, N.J., had meaner sidewalks.

the graffiti watch

Nick's Cafe on North Spring Street tried persuading gang members to confine their graffiti to the lower half of a back wall. A sign directed gang members to the wall, where a second sign implored: "Dogtown, please write below this line." Explained one waitress: "The stuff below the line is easier for us to reach." Mixed results were reported.

LEFT *Anti-graffiti message on storefront in Fairfax district.*

BELOW *This graffiti on wall near Music Center in downtown L.A. began as JESUS SAVES FROM HELL. Someone who apparently had seen too many performances of a popular musical altered it.*

ah, romance...

"Tired of men who don't listen to me," said the personal ad in the L.A. Reader. "Tall, beautiful runway model seeks caring and attentive man; looks unimportant." The ad ended with this warning: "Must be willing to listen to stories of alien abduction."

▼

Fly the (extremely) friendly skies: For $279, a couple could frolic in bed for an hour in the back of a specially outfitted Piper Seneca plane as it buzzed over the Southland. "A lot of people have fantasies about making love in an airplane," said Nick Edgar, proprietor of the Santa Monica-based service. "But you have to be pretty daring to do it on an airliner with 400 other people. This is more intimate. We have a wooden partition between the two pilots and the passenger cabin." Champagne and chocolate-covered strawberries were part of the package.

▼

Those weren't lifeguards that Hermosa Beach police found in a lifeguard shack one night. They were two naked men and two naked women, who invited the officers to join them for "a little orgy." Police booked them for trespass, vandalism and indecent exposure.

▼

Lynda Slagle heard a stylish woman in her 30s say it at a movie screening: "Before I was in therapy, I wanted to be with someone like Warren Beatty in 'Bugsy.' But now after three years of analysis, I'm more interested in meeting someone like Nick Nolte in 'Prince of Tides.'"

▼

And we're not unimpressed: A guy at a Santa Monica bistro used this line to impress the woman seated next to him at the bar: "I think I came from a non-dysfunctional family."

Evidence that the safe-sex campaign is a success? A woman's purse was stolen while she was paying for gasoline in Glassell Park. The purse was found later on the roof of a nearby building. The only thing missing was a pack of condoms.

we'll not be dating him again

A South Bay woman met a visitor from the East in a bar and, against her better judgment, wrote her phone number on a cocktail napkin. He later phoned her and they went out a couple of times. That seemed to be the end of it.

Then one day she received a phone call from a man she didn't know. He said he wanted to thank her for being so courteous, but he needed some additional information.

"What are you talking about?" she asked.

He explained that he was the owner of the car that she had hit in a parking lot. And he thanked her for putting her phone number on a cocktail napkin and leaving it on his windshield.

sometimes it doesn't really work out

Author and renowned relationship expert Barbara De Angelis, the teacher at a Learning Annex seminar entitled "Making Love Work," has been married five times.

▼

Marilyn Stein was inspecting a Brentwood mansion that had been put up for sale because of a divorce. She walked into an upstairs room that was deserted except for an oil portrait of the estranged husband—with a pencil-sized hole punched into his smiling face.

▼

Shortest Hollywood marriage: Rudolph Valentino and actress Jean Acker. She locked the Great Lover out of their honeymoon suite at the Hollywood Hotel six hours after they said their I-Do's on Nov. 5, 1919. Acker later said she simply realized the wedding had been a "mistake."

proposals to be remembered

You couldn't blame Shelley Gilad for being startled by the movie at a Tarzana theater. After all, a character on the screen was speaking to her. It was boyfriend Ron Graening, delivering a 40-second marriage proposal. "Good evening, ladies and gentlemen," it began. "Excuse the brief interruption, but I'd like to speak to the lady I love…" After Gilad recovered from her surprise, she said yes and the audience cheered. Graening, a graphic artist, had taped the short subject at home and arranged to have it shown before the start of the regular feature.

▼

A British Columbia man and his fiancee were picked out of the crowd at Universal Studios and asked to play the lead roles in a wedding commercial about to be taped. They agreed. Near the end of the taping, the man produced an engagement ring and asked her to marry him. She was confused because it looked like the ring she had picked out a year ago. In fact, it was. The "commercial" was a hoax arranged by her husband-to-be as an offbeat way to propose. She said yes, of course. He paid Universal $5,000 for staging the ruse.

▼

For his surprise marriage proposal, Art Streiber wanted to pick a romantic spot where he and his girlfriend spent a lot of time together. So he chose the Santa Monica Freeway. Pulling over at the La

Cabrina Finn

and

Jay Bernstein

are pleased to announce

their marriage

on Saturday, the seventeenth of April

Nineteen hundred and ninety-three

Saint Martin

French West Indies

But where did they cut the cake?

Brea exit, Streiber produced a chilled bottle of champagne from the trunk, knelt on one knee next to the roadway and, ring in hand, proposed to Glynis Costin. She accepted. Said Streiber: "I told her: 'Whenever you pass the La Brea exit, you'll be reminded of this moment.'"

marriage l.a. style

It was your basic wedding ceremony—except for the rings. In rites held at a Hollywood tattoo parlor, bride Laura Stephens and groom Kevin Brady had black rings engraved on their fingers to underscore their commitment. "We stopped the ceremony where you normally exchange the rings," Brady explained. "It took about 10 or 15 minutes to have them tattooed."

▼

CHP Officer John Bavetta and L.A. County Sheriff's Deputy Candace Dean were married at the same romantic spot in La Canada Flintridge where they met a year earlier—the scene of a traffic accident. Dean was responding to a call when her car collided with another, and Bavetta stopped to help.

▼

About to face a judge for scuffling with police, Ulysses Petro was informed that the charge would be reduced to disturbing the peace if he pleaded guilty. Petro was willing to plea bargain under one condition: that the judge marry Petro and his fiancée. His Honor agreed. "Guilty," Petro said. A deputy public defender brought the cake, and the prosecutor took the wedding pictures with his Polaroid.

P.S. Things are Rough! Envelopes are appreciated (full) to pay for this party!!

SELF DEFENSE — Four week marital arts program; 6720 Melrose Ave..

It's taken some couples an entire lifetime.

Notation at the bottom of wedding announcement.

spelchek

The flyer for a medical office said doctors would gladly accept patients **"between ages 40 and 999."**

to your health

Plastic surgeon Robert Kotler of Beverly Hills made no bones about his profession. He handed out business cards containing before and after photos of patients, and ordered up T-shirts with the slogan: "If your face is not becoming to you…you should be coming to us!"

▼

In L.A. taping a talk show, TV host Jon Stewart wanted to see just how health conscious Angelenos really were. He placed a container of Musclebuilder 2500 protein powder next to Arnold Schwarzenegger's star on the Walk of Fame and a carton of Camel cigarettes on a Melrose Avenue sidewalk. The cigarettes were grabbed in less than 10 seconds, but 15 minutes passed before the protein powder was taken.

▼

Sarah Watson was pregnant and past her due date when she walked into Glendale Adventist Hospital to see her husband, Mike, who had just undergone an appendectomy. Suddenly, she felt some pains of her own. The hospital found a bed for her, and she gave birth to a 6-pound, 5-ounce girl. Mike only had to ascend two floors to visit his wife and new daughter.

▼

A luxury hotel in Beverly Hills and another in West Hollywood kept their occupancy rates up by catering to socialites and celebrities recovering from cosmetic surgery. At one hostelry, guests arrived via an underground tunnel to assure privacy. Both offered limo service from doctor's office to hotel—behind tinted windows, of course.

▼

Taking the health fad too far: Thieves broke into UCLA's Wooden Center and carried off four stair-climber exercise machines.

A Fairfax Avenue business called I Scream provided customers a room where they could do just that for a dollar a minute.

And don't do either while driving: Just before Halloween, Beverly Hospital of Montebello issued a set of pumpkin-carving precautions, including: "Don't drink and carve."

A secretary explaining why her doctor boss wouldn't be able to make immediate contact with a caller said: "I'm going to be on vacation Thursday and Friday, and she (the doctor) doesn't ever dial her own phone calls."

▼

A weight loss center in Brentwood used a computer to grill its clients about the underlying causes of their weight problems. The machine posed such questions as "How often do you tell the truth?" and "Does talking about your marriage embarrass you?" Said a spokesman: "We've found that what might not have come out in years of psychotherapy has surfaced for some patients who've responded to the computer's questions."

▼

Tooth tattoos executed by dental ceramist Daniel Materdomini of Woodland Hills have included a New York Yankees logo, a keyboard and the scales of justice (ordered by an attorney). The tiny decorations are printed on porcelain caps, which are then placed over teeth.

▼

When Long Beach Community Hospital opened a new wing next to a drive-in theater, patients had a clear view of the screen below. So arrangements were made with the drive-in to "run a wire up there so they could hear the sound," recalled spokesman Mark Scott. TVs finally replaced the makeshift entertainment system.

In Southern California, even death is temporary.

before HMOs

When a smallpox epidemic broke out in L.A. in 1844, the City Council issued several regulations, author James Guinn noted. Among them: a ban on eating peppers and spices "which stimulate the blood" and a requirement that all residents in good health bathe themselves at least once every eight days.

▼

People called it the "pest farm." It was in Chavez Ravine, in the area now occupied by the Naval and Marine Corps Reserve Center. Irene Dalrymple of Gardena knew firsthand what it was: a hospital for victims of contagious disease.

"There was an outbreak of smallpox in the summer of 1924," she recalled.

"My sister and I and a number of kids from St. Cecilia's grammar school at 42nd and Normandie caught the disease."

Ambulances took them all to the hospital, and "our parents visited us behind a high wire fence across a strip of no-man's-land."

Two weeks later, they were fully recovered.

▼

In the 1860s, when barbers dabbled in other disciplines, A. Meyer of L.A. ran an ad announcing: "Gentlemen will be waited on and have Shaving, Hair-Dressing, and Shampooing prepared in the most luxurious manner, and in the finest style of the art; while Cupping, Bleeding and Teeth-Extracting will also be attended to!"

In case you want to take it out on the road.

The price is OK, but should dentists be doing this?

is this a medical trend?

At the patient's request, six hours of "face sculpturing" by a plastic surgeon was videotaped for future showing. The patient: fashion designer Mr. Blackwell.

A Marina del Rey doctor of deja vu.

▼

Radio talk show host Joe Crummey produced a 30-minute video of his brain operation, including an interview with the surgeon. Said Crummey: "You can look inside my head for $22.50."

are you sure we're alone?

A couple made love on a ridge behind the Hollywood Bowl during the 1993 Playboy Jazz Festival, apparently unaware that hundreds of spectators had binoculars trained on them. One audience member noted that each time the duo "would change whatever they were doing, people would cheer them on."

This double specialty seems appropriate.

▼

Patrolling the skies in KABC's traffic helicopter, reporter Jorge Jarrin looked down to see "a couple in the throes of ecstasy on a blanket in what they thought was a secluded pasture off Mulholland Drive. We were probably only a hundred yards off the ground. The guy jumped up and started doing the one-legged hop, trying to put his pants on." The woman was a bit more relaxed, Jarrin recalled: "She jumped up and started waving to us."

A new service from the Times?

The Church of the Valley in Van Nuys is on Vesper Avenue.

The Cain Professorship at the Claremont School of Theology was named not for Abel's brother, but for a former school president.

The largest crowd ever at the L.A. Coliseum—134,254—gathered in 1963 to see evangelist Billy Graham.

Seems like the message needs a little work.

Drive in and pray: The first place of worship to hold drive-in services was Emmanuel Lutheran Church in North Hollywood, in 1948. Some 120 autos were parked on the church playground and ushers walked from car to car, passing out hymnals and taking collections. The services continued for about two decades.

well, this IS marquee country

The wit and wisdom of messages displayed at Southland churches:

OUR RETIREMENT PLAN IS OUT OF THIS WORLD
(Burbank)

FIRST BAPTIST PARKING ONLY— VIOLATORS WILL BE BAPTIZED
(L.A.)

THE LORD LOVETH A CHEERFUL GIVER. HE ALSO ACCEPTETH FROM A GROUCH
(North Hollywood)

THIS IS YOUR LAST CHANCE TO PRAY BEFORE THE FREEWAY
(Torrance)

FREE FAITH LIFTS EVERY SUNDAY
(Santa Monica)

SINCE A.D. 33
(L.A.)

IF YOU THINK IT'S HOT HERE...
(Venice church during a heat wave)

testimonials

L.A. is a city created by God "so insomniacs in New York would have a place to call in the middle of the night."

−Author Fran Leibowitz

"What's the difference between L.A. and yogurt? Yogurt has an active culture."

−From "Wicked Words," a dictionary of insults

we could

"The whole place smells like an overripe cantaloupe."

−Playwright Neil Simon in "California Suite"

"Thought is barred in this city of dreadful joy."

−Writer Aldous Huxley

do without

"An untidy jumble of human diversity and perversity."

−Columnist George Will

"Nothing is wrong with Southern California that a rise in the ocean level wouldn't cure."

−Mystery novelist Ross Macdonald

"It's as if someone tilted the continent to the west and everything loose slid into Los Angeles."

−Architect Frank Lloyd Wright

"Three million people in the City of Angels, easily half of them up to something they don't want the other half to know."

—From the musical, "City of Angels"

"It's redundant to die in L.A."

—Attributed to Truman Capote in the play, "Tru"

"Horrid, dull, sun-poisoned palms where anemic black rats lived."

—Writer Kate Braverman, describing L.A. palm trees

"I was going to say you'd make a fine wife for somebody if you didn't live in Glendale."

—Character in "Mildred Pierce," by James Cain

"L.A. is the loneliest and most brutal of American cities. New York gets god-awful cold in the winter but there's a feeling of wacky comradeship somewhere in some street. L.A. is a jungle."

—Writer Jack Kerouac in "On the Road"

"A big hard-boiled city with no more personality than a paper cup."

—Mystery writer Raymond Chandler

by any other name...

The long literary tradition of finding new names for Los Angeles has produced: Cuckoo Land (Will Rogers), Moronia (H. L. Mencken), the Queen City of Plastic (Norman Mailer), the Big Orange (Jack Smith), Lozangeles (Herb Caen) and Double Dubuque (H.L. Smith). Oscar Wilde was much kinder, describing the city as "a sort of Naples."

In 1934, visitors to downtown Pershing Square
could borrow library books
for an afternoon of leisure-
ly reading.

history

Translating from the Spanish (welcome to Executioner Hills)...**Celebrity landmarks**, including intersections...Our age-old debate over **how to say El Lay**...The famed gunslinger who became (what else?) a film adviser.

L.A.'s first cemetery, located near the Plaza Church on North Main Street in the early 19th Century, later became a parking lot.

▼

The city's first public golf course opened in 1897 at the corner of Pico Boulevard and Alvarado Street. Tin cups served as holes.

▼

Electric lighting was installed on L.A. streets in 1882 despite complaints that it was hard on the eyes, produced color blindness and optical illusions, was bad for ladies' complexions, and kept chickens awake all night.

▼

Hattem's, a store that leased space to grocers, butchers and bakers, opened at 43rd Street and Western Avenue in 1927. It claimed to be the first to call itself a "supermarket."

▼

The nation's first chinchilla farm was founded in L.A. in 1923. The pioneering creatures were from Peru and Chile.

The former Bullock's Wilshire building, erected in 1929 in a bean field, is considered by some historians to have been the first suburban department store. To lure customers away from downtown stores, the Art Deco landmark built one of the first on-site parking facilities.

Chinese soldiers committed to the overthrow of the Manchu Dynasty trained with the U.S. Army in the L.A. area in the early 1900s and even marched in the Rose Parade one year.

President Millard Fillmore signed a bill admitting California into the union in 1850, but L.A. didn't get the news for weeks. It had no telegraph and no railroad service.

Boston refused to accept shipments of navel oranges from L.A. at the turn of the century, terming the fruit's name "indelicate and immodest."

The first discovery of gold in commercial quantities in California was made in Placerita Canyon near Newhall in 1842.

▼

L.A.'s first drive-in movie opened in the 1930s at the corner of Pico and Westwood Boulevards.

▼

The Crossroads of the World, a series of European-type shops off Sunset Boulevard crowned by a 60-foot-tall spinning globe, is believed to be Southern California's first shopping mall. It opened in 1936.

▼

L.A.'s first rapid transit system was a horse trolley on Spring Street, opened in 1873 by Robert Widney.

▼

Just over a century ago, the four-story Nadeau Hotel at First and Spring Streets became the first building in the city to install an elevator. The city's first escalator is believed to have been installed in Bullock's Department Store at 7th Street and Broadway about 1907.

▼

Edward L. Doheny dug L.A.'s first significant oil well near Glendale Boulevard in 1892. Dug it with a shovel, too.

▼

One of L.A.'s most famous speeches was delivered in 1913 by William Mulholland, head of the city water department. The occasion was the opening of the 233-mile Los Angeles Aqueduct. As water from the distant Owens Valley cascaded into a San Fernando Valley reservoir for the first time, Mulholland said: "There it is, Mr. Mayor. Take it." End of speech.

Mulholland

Historian John Weaver credits pioneer businessman Earle C. Anthony with introducing the taxi cab to L.A. in 1908. Fare was 30 cents for the first half-mile and 20 cents for each additional quarter-mile. "There is no reason," the L.A. Times said at the time, "why a dozen cabs cannot be kept busy here."

▼

Daniel Yergin in his epic book "The Prize" noted this oddity in L.A.'s oil history: After the Signal Hill oil strike in the early 1920s, "the next-of-kin of persons buried in the Sunnyside Cemetery on Willow Street would eventually receive royalty checks for oil drawn out from beneath family grave plots."

▼

In more innocent times, L.A. city directories listed the home addresses of just about everyone, from the mayor to movie stars, authors and evangelists. Here is a sampling of those listings, taken from various directories of earlier years:

Chandler Raymond (Pearl C) writer h4616 Greenwood pl
Cryer George E, Mayor City of Los Angeles, Room 16, City Hall. h530 Shatto pl
Chaney Lon actor h7166 Sunset blvd
Davis James E. Chief of Police 318 W. 1st h786 Micheltorena
De Mille Cecil B Pres Cecil B De Mille Pictures Corp,h4 Laughlin Park
Earp Wyatt mining h4000 1/2 W 17th
Fitzgerald F S hl403 N Laurel ave
Gable Clark actor h608 N Irving blvd
Laurel Stanley actor h3716 S Van Ness
McPherson Aimee S Mrs pastor Angelus Temple hll00 Glendale blvd
Sennett Mack prs Mack Sennett Inc hl41 Westmoreland
Valentino Rudolfo actor h6776 Wedgewood pl

▼

Gambling ships operated in Santa Monica Bay in the 1930s until then-Atty. Gen. Earl Warren declared them the state's "greatest nuisance" and ordered them to shut down. Three obeyed, and had their gambling equipment thrown overboard. But the crew of the fourth ship, the Rex, resisted by turning fire hoses on authorities who tried to board. After an eight-day standoff, the ship's commander surrendered. The Rex was immortalized in the Raymond Chandler novel, "Farewell My Lovely."

miscelLAny

During the late 1950s and early 1960s when Southern California feared an A-bomb attack, backyard fallout shelters cost as much as $5,500 (with phone and toilet) and there was even a line of fallout-shelter clothing, including lead-lined pajamas.

Two of the reasons Orange County withdrew from L.A. County in 1889, according to the book "A Hundred Years of Yesterdays": (1) a stagecoach ride from Anaheim to the county seat in L.A. cost the outlandish price of $6 and (2) the county's only rolled fire hose was kept in L.A.

Crew of the Rex waits with fire hoses to defend ship as a water taxi pulls away.

famous names

Gaylord Wilshire, the developer who laid out the boulevard of the same name before the turn of the century, was also an inventor. He marketed a magnetic collar that supposedly restored gray hair to its original color and cured a variety of ailments. The claims were later disproved.

▼

Gen. George S. Patton, the World War II hero, was born in San Marino and reared in San Gabriel on a ranch owned by his grandfather, Benjamin Wilson, mayor of L.A. in the mid-1800s. Patton's father was L.A. district attorney in the late-1800s. After the general's death in 1945, a window in San Gabriel's Church of Our Saviour was dedicated in his memory and a statue placed on the grounds.

▼

Kellogg Hall on the Cal Poly Pomona campus was the winter home of **W. K. Kellogg**, the Battle Creek, Mich., cereal magnate. Kellogg donated the land now occupied by the university.

▼

After the 1916 death of her father, Grigori Rasputin—sometimes known as the Mad Monk— **Maria Rasputin** moved to the United States, and lived for a time off Sunset Boulevard in Echo Park.

▼

Natives of L.A.: former U.S. Chief Justice **Earl Warren**, costume designer **Edith Head**, two-time presidential nominee **Adlai Stevenson**, Interior Secretary **Bruce Babbit**, astronaut **Sally Ride**, former HUD Secretary **Jack Kemp**, **Iva Toguri D'Aquino** (the notorious Tokyo Rose), choreographer **Busby Berkeley**, actor **Leo Carrillo** and actress **Marilyn Monroe**.

tales of old l.a.

In 1890, the Santa Fe Railway offered a free train ticket "from anywhere east of the Rocky Mountains" to anyone who bought property in Lordsburg, now La Verne. The catch was that the purchaser had to spend at least $500.

▼

The Los Feliz district of L.A. took its name from Domingo Los Feliz, a wealthy landowner who was murdered by his wife's lover in 1836. Los Feliz Boulevard south of Griffith Park follows the path once used by the rancher and his cowhands.

▼

The Drum Barracks Museum in Wilmington is a reminder of the Civil War. A few thousand Union troops were stationed at the barracks during that conflict, partly out of fears that Confederate sympathizers in L.A. might lead a revolt.

▼

Soon after Central Park (now Pershing Square) was dedicated in downtown L.A. in 1866, the city was forced to surround it with a picket fence to keep out stray horses and cattle.

▼

It's one of many cities along the San Bernardino Freeway now. But a plaque outside the Museum of History in El Monte notes that the town was the last stop on another thoroughfare—the Santa Fe Trail.

▼

El Monte had such a large population of Southerners during the Civil War that a Confederate flag was raised in the town square each time there was news of a Rebel victory.

from an 1886 l.a. visitors guide:

- "Sunstrokes are unknown save on the desert."

- "The inhabitants do not wear arsenals nor shoot at the drop of a handkerchief. The Apaches are 800 miles away."

- "For a short time after the rain, the streets are muddy. Three days of sunshine makes them all right."

- "Los Angeles is the Chicago of California."

From historian Jim Rawls in his book "California Dreaming":

When William Wallace, the owner of the Los Angeles Star, sold the newspaper in 1856, he wrote that he was getting out of town because "the flush times of the pueblo, the day of large pocketbooks, are past." L.A., he predicted, would be characterized by "picayunes, bad liquor, rags and universal dullness, when neither pistol shots nor dying groans" would have any impact and "when earthquakes would hardly turn men in their beds!'"

▼

Thirty-five vigilante hangings were recorded in L.A. when it was a small but wild pueblo in the 1800s.

▼

In the 1880s, the sound of five or six revolver shots in L.A. signaled that a fire had broken out. That number was favored, a historian noted, because fewer shots probably would be dismissed as a mere difference of opinion between two citizens.

▼

L.A. boasted 110 saloons in 1870, or about one for every 50 residents.

and no area codes

L.A.'s first phone book, published in 1882, contained 92 numbers, including those of 22 residents, eight doctors, four horse stables, one real estate man and no lawyers. Some of the easy-to-remember listings:

Southern Pacific Railroad, 1.
Evergreen Cemetery, 69.
USC, 58.
Police, 30.
Pico House, 9.
Los Angeles Club, 38.

the fastest guns in l.a.

In 1929, an old gunfighter died peacefully in his sleep in L.A. A lawman, gambler and miner, he had made his name in places like Dodge City and Tombstone. He retired in L.A., where he gave advice to filmmakers shooting early Westerns and raced horses at Exposition Park and elsewhere. At the age of 70, he learned to drive an automobile. He lived out his final days quietly in a house at 4000 ½ W. 17th Street, near the corner of Venice and Crenshaw Boulevards. Perhaps that's why the L.A. Times relegated his death, at age 80, to an inside page. An understated exit for Wyatt Earp.

▼

Emmett Dalton, a member of the infamous Dalton Gang, moved to the Los Feliz area in the 1920s after serving 15 years in prison for attempting to rob a Kansas bank. In L.A., the onetime outlaw found a legal way to separate people from their money: he became a real estate agent. Dalton lived at 1928 Hillhurst Avenue for a time. He died in 1937 at the age of 66.

Earp in his later years.

▼

By the time he was jailed on murder charges in L.A. in 1874, desperado Tiburcio Vasquez had become such a celebrity that a local merchant took out newspaper ads declaring: "Tiburcio Vasquez says that Mendell Meyer has the finest and most complete stock of dry goods and clothing." While he was awaiting execution, a play based on his life opened downtown. Vasquez volunteered to portray himself, but authorities nixed the deal. Vasquez was later hanged, but not forgotten. A geological formation near Newhall that served as his hideout was named after him — the Vasquez Rocks. So was a high school in the town of Agua Dulce.

where they got their names:

Hawaiian Gardens took its name from a bamboo-and-thatched-roof food stand that served travelers along the old Coyote Creek Trail in the 1920s.

▼

El Segundo (in English, "the second") was the site of Standard Oil's second refinery in California.

▼

Lynwood was named for Lynn Wood Sessions, the wife of a local dairy owner.

▼

In 1919, Tarzan creator Edgar Rice Burroughs purchased 550 acres of pastoral land in what later came to be known as **Tarzana**, in the San Fernando Valley.

▼

Burbank, christened in honor of Dr. David Burbank, is the only city in L.A. County to be named after a dentist.

how to say el lay

The correct pronunciation of Los Angeles has confused newcomers and visitors for decades.

The Chamber of Commerce issued this helpful ditty in the late 1800s: "The Lady would remind you, please/Her name is not Lost Angie Lees." In the early 1900s, the Los Angeles Times printed a daily reminder to use the traditional Spanish version: loss *AHNG-hayl-ais*. The Times' guide didn't stop President Theodore Roosevelt from saying loss *AN-gee-lees* on one visit. Mayor Sam Yorty later offered a different variation: *loss ANG-uh-lus*.

A special commission appointed to study the problem finally declared the official pronunciation to be: *loss-AN-juh-less*.

translation, please

Sometimes, it seems that Southern Californians have chosen Spanish and Indian names more for their mellifluous sound than for their meaning. Consider the following translations:

Communities
Verdugo Hills: Executioner Hills
Laguna Niguel: Chigger Lagoon
Calabasas: Pumpkins
Saugus: Mouth
Cabazon: Misshapen Head.

Streets
Las Pulgas Road: Fleas Road
Puerco Canyon Road: Pig Canyon Road
La Tijera Boulevard: Scissors Boulevard.
La Cienega Boulevard: The Swamp Boulevard
El Vago Street: Vagrant Street

La Crescenta sounds Spanish but is an invented word. Its creator was pioneer resident Benjamin Briggs, who was inspired by "three crescent-shaped formations" visible from his home, according to the book "California Place Names."

La Mirada translates as The Glance. According to legend, railroad officials came up with the name because a passer-by could take in the whole town with just one glance.

Azusa, the story goes, was so named because it had "everything in the USA, from A to Z." Actually, it derived its name from an Indian village. Azusa translates roughly as "skunk hill."

Las Tunas State Beach, south of Malibu, was originally named by Spanish explorers. But they had an inland feature, not fish, in mind. Tuna is Spanish for the fruit of the prickly pear cactus.

A literal translation of two familiar names:

The La Brea Tar Pits –
The The Tar Tar Pits.

The Los Angeles Angels –
The The Angels Angels.

civic pride dept.

A sampling of community slogans in the Southland, some still in use, others only a memory:

Together We're the Best. L.A. (Los Angeles)
Twenty-Nine Churches, No Jails (Bellflower)
The Aristocrat of the Beaches (Hermosa Beach)
Harbor of the Air (Inglewood)
The Freeway City (Gardena)
The Most on the Coast (Long Beach)
Tan Your Hide in Oceanside (Oceanside)
P.S., I Love You (Palm Springs)
I Love B.S. (Borrego Springs)
Where the Hell is Norco? (Norco)
Celery Capital of the World (Lomita)
Heart of Screenland (Culver City)
Home of the American Olive (Pomona)
Home of the Apollo (Downey)
Hay Capital of the World (Paramount)
The Fastest-Growing City in America (Glendale)

the many uses of the l.a. river

• Scene of more TV and movie chases than any other waterway. Emilio Estevez raced along its pavement in "Repo Man" and wacky weatherman Steve Martin tooled to work on the riverbed in "L.A. Story."

• During World War II, used by Army trucks to rush munitions to the sea. With the Harbor and Long Beach Freeways yet to be built, the dry riverbed was the fastest route to the harbor.

• The setting for a multimedia performance entitled "Mother Ditch." Dancers waded into the muck under the Glendale Boulevard bridge in Atwater.

• A training ground for city bus drivers. They practiced maneuvering their big vehicles along the paved riverbed.

just don't call it olliewood

The Hollywood sign originally said "Hollywoodland" and was erected on Mt. Lee in 1923 by a land developer as an outdoor advertisement that could be seen for miles. The "land" portion was lopped off later by the Hollywood Chamber of Commerce to give the sign more universal appeal. In 1932, a 24-year-old actress named Peg Entwistle, apparently upset over bad reviews for her first big film, climbed atop the letter "H" and jumped to her death. When the dilapidated letters had to be replaced in 1978, several celebrities pitched in to purchase new ones. Among the biggest donors were Alice Cooper, Hugh Hefner, Gene Autry and Andy Williams, each of whom contributed the cost of constructing one letter ($27,777.77). The sign is sometimes altered temporarily by pranksters ("Hollyweed" was the work of a pro-marijuana group and "Olliewood" paid tribute to Oliver North).

Hollywood sign before it
was shortened in 1945.

vernon's glory days

There was a time early in the century when Vernon, an industrial city just south of Los Angeles, was one of the hot spots in Southern California.

It boasted a baseball park and a Pacific Coast League team, a boxing arena with world-class matches and Jack Doyle's Saloon, which claimed the distinction of housing the "Longest Bar in the World."

Prohibition pretty much spelled the end of Vernon's night life, though it went out in a big way. The night before the nation went dry, more than 60 bartenders patrolled the 100-foot-long bar at Doyle's, doling out drinks to an estimated 1,000 customers in what was the ultimate Last Call.

built for the year 2000

The Bradbury Building is a century old landmark at 3rd Street and Broadway that is celebrated for its wrought-iron staircases, bird-cage elevators and skylit courtyard. George Wyman, the building's designer, was said to have been inspired by a contemporary novelist who described the typical office building of the year 2000 as "a vast hall full of light, received not alone from the windows on all sides but from the dome."

paradise paved

A Great Western Bank stands where celebrities like F. Scott Fitzgerald, John Barrymore and Marlene Dietrich once frolicked at a collection of bungalows known as the Garden of Allah on Sunset Boulevard. Writer Robert Benchley was said to have fallen into a pool there and declared: "Get me out of these wet clothes and into a dry martini." Though bulldozed in 1959, the Garden survives in a sense: a model is housed under a glass bubble in the bank. And an old Joni Mitchell lyric ("They paved paradise and put up a parking lot") honored the Garden as well.

talk about a late train...

Cars on the historic Angels Flight railway always chugged along at a slow pace, but no one ever thought they would fall 27 years behind schedule. When the 300-foot railway was dismantled in 1969 to make room for the Bunker Hill renewal project, the city promised it would be running again in two years. The cars went into storage and remained there until the line went back into operation in 1996, about a half block south of its original location next to the 3rd Street tunnel.

does this sound familiar?

Nice to know the city hasn't changed all that much: The May 4, 1927, issue of the Los Angeles Illustrated Daily News contained articles about:

- A conference to reduce traffic accidents in Los Angeles.
- Plans for a sanitarium for narcotics addicts.
- A meat market owner complaining that doctors were telling their patients not to eat too much meat.
- A cigar-smoker saying he was discriminated against.

A park with a tough stand on crime? Actually, the name dates back almost half a century, according to La Crescenta librarian Mary Jones. Actor Dennis Morgan, honorary mayor at the time, wanted to get kids off the streets. He felt "that any child who had to play in the street had two strikes against him, and the third strike could be getting hit by a car," Jones said. So Morgan organized a series of ballgames with celebrities and star players that helped raise the funds to build Two Strike Park.

celebrity landmarks

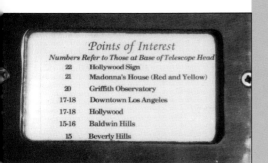

Does the Material Girl know about this?

Burbank renamed a park in honor of Johnny Carson, longtime "Tonight Show" host whose NBC broadcasts originated in that city.

Sorry we missed the dedication ceremony.

Steve Martin Gallery, L.A. County Museum of Art. Named for the actor, a major donor. Martin roller-skated through the museum in the film, "L.A. Story."

State beach parks between Santa Monica and the Ventura County line. Named for comedian **Will Rogers**, Western star **Leo Carrillo** and actor **Dan (Hoss) Blocker**.

Lou Costello Jr. Youth Center, Boyle Heights. It was built with funds that the comic actor raised with his partner, Bud Abbott.

Also:

Jerry Lewis Neuromuscular Research Center, UCLA

Jules Stein Eye Institute, UCLA

George Lucas Instructional Center, USC

Anthony Quinn Library, East Los Angeles

William Hart High School, Newhall

Cary Grant Pavilion, Hollywood Park

Michael Landon Community Center, Malibu

Hackett Avenue, Lakewood (named for Buddy Hackett)

Sidney Sheldon Gallery, L.A. County Museum of Art

Harold Lloyd Motion Picture Sound Stage, USC

Steven Spielberg Music Scoring Stage, USC

Ritchie Valens Park, Pacoima

Jerry Garcia Suite, Beverly Prescott Hotel

Richard and Karen Carpenter Performing Arts Center, Cal State Long Beach

Michael Jackson Auditorium, Gardner Street School, Hollywood

Dr. Gene Scott Diving Tower, Rose Bowl Aquatic Center

statues
in unlikely places

Famed aviator **Amelia Earhart** in North Hollywood Park. She was a resident of North Hollywood before disappearing in 1937.

Actress **Myrna Loy** at Venice High School. She posed for it as a student there.

French heroine **Joan of Arc** in Chinatown. Her statue stands outside the Pacific Alliance Medical Center, formerly the French Hospital.

*Actor **James Dean** at the Griffith Observatory. Scenes from "Rebel Without a Cause" were filmed there.*

celebrity intersections

The L.A. City Council renamed Alden Drive as Gracie Allen Drive so that it would intersect with George Burns Road near Cedars-Sinai Medical Center.

In Beverly Hills, Gregory Way crosses Peck Drive.

981-8885
CONTRACTORS
LICENSE
SCHOOL
3rd FLOOR

Park In Rear

ONE WAY

disasters

An ironic casualty of the Northridge quake.

Earthquake: A list that may cause you to lose some sleep…

Riot: the priest and Ava Gardner's pantaloons…

Drought: if there's no water for grass, green gravel will do just fine…

Fire: some of the dumbest 911 calls.

northridge quake, 1994

Notice posted on a house that had partially slid down a hillside in Pacific Palisades: "For sale. No appointment necessary. Just needs TLC…and a bulldozer."

▼

Motorists gridlocked on San Fernando Road because of quake-damaged highways heard this unusual offer over the public address system of a passing Los Angeles police car: "Does anybody need to go to the bathroom? We will take you to the bathroom and we will return you to your car." Several grateful motorists agreed to be taken into temporary custody.

▼

Thank you, looters: When Carol Schatz bought her Japanese-style house in Beverly Hills years ago, she made a mental note to get rid of the two stone Buddhas in the front yard. Later, she decided they were so heavy it wasn't worth the trouble. Then the quake struck, sending one of the Buddhas down a hill and into the street where it struck the car of her husband, Fred. He left the stone figure sitting on the curb, and within an hour someone had stolen it. When last heard from, Fred was considering moving the other Buddha to the same spot.

Some post-quake humor.

Next to a "For Sale" sign on a house damaged in the quake was this hand-lettered notice: "Some Assembly Required."

▼

As an aftershock rumbled through Ed Debevic's, a 1950s-style diner in Beverly Hills, a waitress wearing period garb yelled: "God, I don't wanna die dressed this way!"

▼

"I Was Looking at the Ceiling and Then I Saw the Sky" was the title of an opera inspired by the Northridge quake.

▼

A gorilla at the L.A. Zoo was so stressed that she had to be put on Valium.

this list may cause you to lose some sleep

One bit of folklore holds that earthquakes are more likely to hit near sunrise or sunset when the gravitational tug of the sun upon the Earth is strongest. Whatever the reason(s), most of Southern California's most important quakes have adhered to a morning/evening schedule:

1. Tejon (7.7+ magnitude), 1857, about 8 a.m.
2. Northwest L.A. (6.0+), 1893, 11:40 a.m.
3. Santa Barbara (6.3), 1925, 6:42 a.m.
4. Long Beach (6.3), 1933, 5:54 p.m.
5. Tehachapi (7.7), 1952, 4:52 a.m.
6. Sylmar (6.6), 1971, 6 a.m.
7. Whittier (5.9), 1987, 7:42 a.m.
8. Sierra Madre (5.8), 1991, 7:43 a.m.
9. Landers (7.4), 1992, 4:58 a.m.
10. Big Bear (6.5), 1992, 8 a.m.
11. Northridge (6.8), 1994, 4:31 a.m.

Wry humor after the Northridge quake

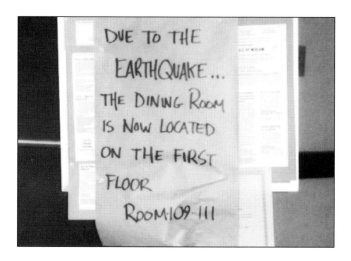

some people have no sense of humor

When the Sierra Madre earthquake of 1991 struck, supervisors and managers in the RTD's offices picked up their red emergency phones and heard these taped instructions: "We are all doomed. Drop your pants and kiss your ass goodby." RTD officials termed the stunt "a poor practical joke" and suspended the culprit for a week.

▼

West Hills physician Ron Baum chose an earthquake message for his personalized license plate: **W8N4BG1**. "It's just a joke, but it shocks some of our friends from out of state," Baum said. "They say earthquakes aren't something to mess with, sort of like it's bad luck even to mention them." Oddly enough, many local drivers give W8N4BG1 the thumbs-up sign. "They seem to think we're referring to the lottery," Baum explained.

A quake strong enough to move the Atlantic west.

l.a. riots, 1992

While buildings still smoldered and the National Guard patrolled the streets, a T-shirt entrepreneur was already hawking shirts that read: "My Mom Went Looting in South-Central L.A. and All I Got Was This Lousy T-Shirt."

I WAS NOT A JUROR.
SIMI VALLEY, CA

Looters at a computer store in Koreatown left their parked car at the curb with the engine running. But a passing resident foiled their getaway by turning off the ignition and tossing the keys out of sight while the looters were still inside the store.

▼

It was particularly ironic that rioters gutted Glasser Bros. Bail Bonds, a 71-year-old downtown landmark. Owner Gary Glasser set up a temporary office elsewhere and was back in business within hours—bailing out many of the persons arrested during the rioting.

▼

Bookkeeper Sheri Watts found herself in the midst of the riot zone but nearly out of gas. She pulled into a service station and discovered to her horror that she had no money. "Then," said Watts, who is white, "this black guy came up to my car. He wasn't dressed very well. I pulled out my Mace. He looked at me and said, 'What are you doing here?' I told him. He pulled out a couple of crumpled dollar bills and change and said, 'Put this in your gas tank and go home now!'" Watts added: "I remember he said, 'Usually I have to ask people for

Post-riot bumper sticker took a dim view of Simi Valley jury that acquitted police in first Rodney King trial.

money,' so he must have been a panhandler. They say this is the City of Angels and I guess he was my angel."

▼

A distraught young man handed a bag to Father Robert Fambrini, pastor at Blessed Sacrament Catholic Church in Hollywood, and confessed that he had looted the lingerie museum at Frederick's of Hollywood. Now he wanted to return what he had taken but was afraid to go back to the store. So it was up to Fambrini to return the stolen merchandise: a bra belonging to actress Katey Sagal (of TV's "Married with Children") and the pantaloons of the late actress Ava Gardner.

l.a. drought, 1988-93

When a fire hydrant burst on Wilshire Boulevard near Westwood, passerby Ken Rogers noticed BMWs, Jaguars and other cars going out of their way to take advantage of the free wash. "They would veer to their right to get to the water and then they'd go through very slowly," Rogers said. "I guess that's what you'd expect in a drought."

▼

Artist Dominic Stefano of View Heights was determined to make his front yard green again despite a no-watering rule. He dyed five tons of gravel that color and spread it over his brown lawn. Four neighbors liked the effect so much that they did the same. "It looks just like dichondra," observed one.

▼

When a trash truck backed over a fire hydrant in the Hollywood Hills, neighbors flocked to the scene. Said resident Dietrich Nelson: "There were people out there in suits and dresses and nightgowns, scooping up water and pouring it on their lawns and flower beds."

fire watch

Two of the Dumbest 911 Emergency Calls: (1) The woman who called from a hospital and said she couldn't get anyone to get her ice. The dispatcher advised her to use the nurses' call button. (2) The man who wanted help opening a locked apartment door. Why? "Deliver food, Chinese food," the caller said. "You need the Fire Department to let you in so you can deliver Chinese food?" the dispatcher inquired. "Yes," came the reply. Then the delivery man hung up.

▼

Most colorful thank you: After a devastating fire swept Topanga, this sign addressed to firefighters was erected in front of a surviving house: "You came, you saw, you kicked ass."

▼

Allen Emerson of Topanga, head of the area's volunteer arson watch, had to change residences after his house burned down while he was away.

DEAR HOMEOWNER
ATTACHED PLEASE FIND 50¢
FOR THE COKE WE TOOK FROM
YOUR FRIDGE. THE HOUSE IS A
LITTLE SMOKY, AND YOUR DECK'S
A GONER BUT OTHERWISE OK
THANKS, WE REALLY NEEDED IT.
L.A SHERIFF.

PS. THANK GOD YOU HAD YOUR HOSE HOOKED UP!

At least his notes weren't singed: Jeff Bliss, public information director of Pepperdine University, had to delay his speech to colleagues on the subject, "Communicating in a Crisis." The cause: a brush fire that threatened the campus.

Or call the fire department: Message from the scene of a fire, overheard on Los Angeles Fire Department radio frequency: "Will you contact the firefighter who's in quarters and tell him to turn the oven off?"

After hosing down the flames that threatened a house evacuated during Malibu fire, two thirsty but scrupulous sheriff's deputies left this note behind. The grateful homeowners managed to learn their identity and honored them with a dinner.

the apocalypse file

Southern California is practically synonymous with Doomsday. Here are a few final moments we've survived:

June 16, 1994 — Prophesied by a poltergeist who appeared in the rear view mirrors of drivers on Pacific Coast Highway, according to an urban folk tale. True believers said police had to stop motorists who began driving erratically after the spirit told them a massive earthquake was coming.

May 8, 1993 — Based on psychics who quoted Nostradamus, the 16th century seer. A Santa Monica store called UFO Excursions shut down, leaving a phone recording that explained "killer quakes are about to strike California."

October 17, 1992 — Announced by a Jamaican clairvoyant during an L.A. press conference. "I have an antenna behind each ear," he revealed, "and they throb when an earthquake is coming."

January 22, 1991 — Picked by a geologist because of a larger-than-usual number of missing-animal reports in the L.A. Times classified section.

March 8, 1982 — Predicted by publisher of an astrological magazine in India. Positions of planets would trigger an earthquake, leaving L.A. submerged under water.

June 9, 1980 — Picked by a Hollywood evangelist who undermined his credibility by showing up late for his own press conference. He explained that he had overslept.

Charlton Heston and Monica Lewis trying to make it through "Earthquake."

February 12, 1969—Readers of the book, "The Last Days of the Late, Great State of California," settled on this date. It also inspired a song by the rock group Shango, with these lyrics: "Do you know the swim? You better learn quick, Jim/Those who don't know the swim/Better sing the hymn."

Nowhere is L.A. more disaster-prone than in the movies:

War of the Worlds (1953): Martian invasion destroys City Hall.

Earthquake (1974): The Big One ruins Charlton Heston's day, leveling Capitol Records tower and rest of the city.

The Day of the Locust (1975): A mob lays waste to human life and Hollywood Boulevard at movie premiere.

Alligator (1980): Sewer-dwelling reptile, driven mad by pollutants, eats several citizens near Echo Park Lake .

Blade Runner (1982): Killer androids cavort in year 2019 in an L.A. tormented by never-ending acid rain and haze.

Miracle Mile (1989): Only the tar pits are left after nuclear war hits Wilshire Boulevard.

Alien Nation (1993 TV movie): Hairless humanoids from outer space crash in Mojave Desert take up residence in Hollywood. No one notices.

Independence Day (1996): Seemingly friendly space aliens turn deadly, leveling several cities including L.A. (and poor City Hall again).

"Escape from L.A." (set for 1996 release): It's the year 2012 and quake-ravaged L.A. is now an island and, well, the title tells the rest.

In the 1970s, street signs were more expressive— and optimistic.

driving

God is a licensed driver, and other tales of the DMV...**Vanity plates** that spelled trouble...World's toughest meter maids...Bulletins from the **parking wars**...The errant golf ball and other **freeway tales**...How we used to drive.

An L.A. man received a phone call from his insurance carrier, the Auto Club. "Was that your voice on the answering machine?" the Auto Club rep asked.

Taken aback, the man said it was. But why did the Auto Club want to know? Well, the rep explained, some people are untruthful when they state on their insurance forms that they're the only drivers in their household.

"What if I had David Letterman's voice on my answering machine?" the man asked. "Would I have to pay for his insurance, too?"

"No," the Auto Club rep answered. "But we would question you about that."

Official membership card in the Auto Club was issued to a mischievous Angeleno who used this unlikely name when responding to a mailed invitation to join the club. He wondered if anyone would notice. They didn't.

▼

Drive-by humor: Two automobile drivers whose cars had collided at 2nd and Spring Streets weren't exactly cheered by an MTA bus passing by. Speaking into his PA system, the bus driver blared at them: "You should have taken the b-u-u-s-s-s! You should have taken the bu-u-u-s-s!"

▼

This fish story was confirmed by South Pasadena police: A motorist was heading down Huntington Drive with a small aquarium in his front seat and a bucket of tropical fish in the back. "One of the fish jumped out of the bucket and went up into the front seat," Officer Mike Neff said. "This startled him, and he took his mind off his driving and started reaching for the fish to put it back in the bucket. Unfortunately, he drove up on a center median and hit a tree head-on." Rescuers put as many of the fish back in the bucket as they could, shoved the bucket into the ambulance, and sent fish and dazed motorist to the hospital together. No one was seriously injured.

▼

Police arrested a motorist in Los Angeles after his car plowed through two doors and a wall and entered...the Total Experience nightclub.

▼

An out-of-control car hit Anthony Manzella's BMW one night while it was parked—inside his garage, with the garage door down. "My wife and I were in the kitchen when we heard this crash," said Manzella. "We went to check—and there was an old Datsun with its nose sticking into our garage." Police arrested the apparently drunk driver.

▼

Spit happens: Two motorists were arguing after a near-collision near the downtown corner of 5th and Hope Streets. One was driving a late-model Lexus, the other a battered old coupe. Suddenly, the driver of the coupe performed the ultimate act of disrespect toward a fellow motorist— he spit on the Lexus. Its pin-striped driver whirled and said to the assembled crowd in disbelief: "Did you see what he did? Did you see what he did?" And he began taking names and addresses of witnesses to the spitting.

▼

A trucker hit a street person's shopping cart in Glendale, then alighted from his rig to argue over who was at fault. While the two were jawing, an Amtrak train crashed into the truck. Then the transient hit the truck driver with a rock and scurried away. And how was your day?

As Melissa Grant of Pacific Palisades tried to throw her chewing gum out the car window one night, a sterling silver ring flew off her finger and into the median strip of the Santa Monica Freeway. She and a girlfriend returned the next day to search for the ring on foot—until CHP Officers Richard Sigler and Joseph Dixon happened by, and ordered them off the freeway. But the story had a happy ending: the officers themselves then took up the search and found the ring, still in the median.

▼

Caltrans tried to persuade other states through which Interstate 10 passes to join in dedicating the roadway to a famed Italian navigator. They all refused, but Caltrans went ahead anyway. Hence a sign alongside the Santa Monica Freeway, telling motorists they are traversing the Christopher Columbus Transcontinental Highway.

▼

Portions of a Toyota test track in Japan were built with uneven surfaces to create tough driving conditions. Naturally, L.A. was honored with one stretch. Autoweek magazine reported this comment from a Toyota official as he drove some American visitors over an especially bumpy section: "Here we are in the United States, on Interstate 91 and the Harbor Freeway."

two questions most asked of traffic reporters

1. What is a SigAlert? It's a broadcast warning to motorists of a serious traffic jam expected to last at least half an hour. The term is a tribute to Loyd Sigmon, a pioneering executive at KMPC who originated the concept in the 1950s.
2. What is the No. 1 lane? It's the fast lane, closest to the center divider.

dropping in at the dmv

A Duarte youth appearing at the Department of Motor Vehicles office in Covina for a driving test got a big demerit before he even started. The examiner became suspicious because the youth's car had no license plates. A computer check showed the car was stolen; the young man was arrested on suspicion of grand theft auto.

▼

The publicist for David Jamison, author of a book on how to fight parking tickets, listed among Jamison's credits: "Former California driver's license examiner. He gave driving tests to Madonna and Muhammad Ali."

▼

When the DMV put a picture of the Mona Lisa on a mock driver's license as part of a publicity campaign, it had to use the name "Mona Liza Smith" to avoid confusion with real people. At the time, 17 Californians had licenses bearing the name, "Mona Lisa."

Driving examiner Ramona Gonzales had already decided to flunk the novice behind the wheel for failing to change lanes properly. But the worst maneuver in the test was yet to come. The unlucky driver, a 28-year-old woman, was turning into the parking lot of the Department of Motor Vehicles headquarters in Glendale when the car suddenly accelerated, crashing into the building. Said Gonzales, who suffered a sprained wrist: "We didn't even get to the parking part of the test." The failed driver was tearful but uninjured.

---

17. This sign means:
    Divided highway ahead .... ☒
    Side road ahead on right .... ☐
    Fewer lanes ahead .... ☐
    Crossroad intersects the main road .... ☐

Judging by the illustration on this DMV driving test, the correct answer must be, "You're driving in England or Japan."

A lot of people say their driver's license photos don't do them justice, but Santa Fe Springs engineer Shan Treanor had a better case than most. When his new license arrived in the mail, it bore the picture of a woman wearing earrings. He wasn't the only one to get a license with someone else's image on it. Marie Ungles of Whittier was sent "a license with my name, etc., but a picture of a man with a mustache." A DMV spokesman explained that the agency had run into "some problems" producing its new, hard-to-counterfeit licenses.

as a matter of fact officer, i DO own the road

You just never know who you're going to see driving in L.A. Take, for example, the Santa Monica man whose license identified him as "Jesus Christ" and the Hollywood driver who was licensed simply as "God."

As you might expect, both had perfect driving records, according to the Department of Motor Vehicles. But neither seemed especially omnipotent: the DMV said both had to wear eyeglasses while on the road.

An agency spokesman said motorists "may legally use any name as long as the intent is not to defraud."

The two men were also registered to vote in L.A. County. Jesus was listed as a Democrat. But God, of course, was a Republican.

God is also a registered voter.

REGISTRAR-RECORDER

	P		NAME(LAST,SUF,FIRST,MI)
ESTR. U C	TXN-D	REG-D O	NAME(LAST,SUF,FIRST,MI)
4050051A	CANC-3	081994	GOCZAL RICHARD L
9000240A	102188	101188	GOD
9016297A	021790	063088	GODA ALAN F
9001306A	110984	011472	GODA ALEXANDER L
9005624B	CANC-2	030893	GODA ANN M

the way we used to drive

What may have been L.A.'s earliest gas station opened at Grand Avenue and Washington Boulevard in 1912 and charged 8 cents a gallon.

▼

A 1916 example of motoring ingenuity, as reported by the Auto Club magazine, Touring Topics: "A man with a self-steering Ford was arrested in L.A. recently…The car, which was equipped with a device to make any Ford keep the street without the attention of the driver, ran true to form, but the trouble was that it required the whole street to operate it."

▼

John Wilcock in the guidebook, "Los Angeles," quoted an L.A. police captain telling the Board of Supervisors: "The practice of making love on the highways is becoming alarmingly prevalent. In many cases, it is flagrantly open." The captain made that report in 1921.

▼

Motorcar speed limits at the turn of the century in L.A. were 8 m.p.h. in residential sections, 6 m.p.h. in the business district and 4 m.p.h. at unmarked intersections.

▼

Inventor J. Philip Erie drove the first gasoline-powered automobile through Los Angeles in 1897. Reviews were mixed. The L.A. Times reported that the four-cylinder Erie and Sturgis Gasolene Carriage zipped over "the awful Sixth Street pavement" and the "chuckholes innumerable on Main Street" so smoothly that "passengers scarcely felt any motion at all." The Sunday Herald, however, complained that the jalopy "barely moved" faster than foot traffic and didn't come close to its advertised top speed of 25 m.p.h.

A driving school with a sense of humor.

OPPOSITE *In 1920, downtown traffic was really congested, if we believe this cartoon strip from the L.A. Times. A driver could fall in love (pippin was slang for "a person much admired"), get married, raise a family, grow a beard and reach old age—all while traveling a mere six blocks.*

In the 1920s, wooden-sided Fords were often used to drive passengers to and from train stations. That is how the vehicles came to be known as station wagons, according to Westways magazine.

▼

The city's first traffic signal was installed in 1920 at Adams Boulevard and Figueroa Street and behaved "like a cross between a railroad semaphore and an alarm clock," according to one account. "As the arm moved from the 'Go' to 'Stop,' a bell jingled merrily in the crow's nest."

▼

"It is quite true that there are too many traffic accidents in Los Angeles," said a writer in the Auto Club News. "Never have I been in a city where I saw so many motor drivers who appeared tense, frightened or even partially dazed." The piece appeared in 1920.

▼

In early days, L.A.'s thoroughfares were laid out so that each "avenue" (such as Western) would run north-south and each "street" would run east-west (Pico Boulevard was originally Pico Street).

but did he accept validations?

When Andrew Pansini opened his downtown business in 1917, his friends scoffed. "People told him that no one was ever going to pay to have their car parked," recalled his daughter, Mary La Haye. And certainly not for the outrageous sum of 5 cents per day.

Pansini, an Italian immigrant, is generally credited with opening the city's first parking lot. He got the idea, said La Haye, after noticing "a peg-legged man watching cars on the street. People would throw him dimes when they came back to their cars." Pansini acquired property at the corner of 4th Street and Olive Avenue and the rest is history.

messages on wheels

The car on the Santa Monica Freeway carried a vanity plate that said: **DEB'N'ART**. On the plate frame was this rhyming update: "Are Now Apart." Deb appeared to have won custody of the automobile.

▼

Very restless people live here: The license plates on two cars parked on a tranquil, tree-lined street in Pacific Palisades: **H8 W8N** and **H8 W8EN**.

▼

So there will be no confusion: Spotted on the Westside — an automobile with a license plate that said, **H8 MY X** and a bumper sticker that declared: "I Love My Parrot."

▼

Are We a Bit Defensive? Observed in Echo Park — a car with the license plate **YME OFSR**.

▼

One motorist who wasn't being tailgated or cut off on the Ventura Freeway on a busy morning was the dressed-for-success woman in a late model Porsche with the license plate: **LAWSUIT**.

A group of nuns disembarked from a van with the license plate: **NUNSRUS**.

▼

Upset over bumper stickers that use vulgar language? How refreshing to see a gardener's truck with a message that said: "Fertilizer Happens."

▼

A big rig on the Artesia Freeway didn't exactly exude the romance of the road with license plates on its truck and trailer that said, respectively, **DAMNTRK** and **DAMNTLR**.

▼

On the back of the motorcyclist's leather jacket was a drawing of a fist clutching a wad of cash. The lettering below read: "Accountant from Hell."

▼

Dept. of Competing Desires: After a car was sighted in L.A. with a **BAK2NY** license plate, another was seen in Ventura with a plate that said **BACK2LA**.

▼

Two vanity license plates that have something to say about mudslides in Malibu: **MLBUMUD** and **PCHCLSD**.

▼

License plate frame on a black sports car in East L.A.: "I'm fun, single and HIV-negative."

▼

San Francisco columnist Herb Caen was cheered by the discovery of "another lost soul on the Santa Monica Freeway." The cause of his glee: a license plate reading **YMINLA**.

Pray for them: A Honda Civic on the Ventura Freeway sported a mangled rear fender that had been badly repainted, a crumpled front fender, and doors with assorted dents and scratches. The car's nameplate read: "Hallelujah School of Driving."

▼

The gray-haired man was grimly hunched over the wheel as he puttered along at 35 m.p.h. in the 65 m.p.h. traffic on the Santa Monica Freeway. A woman sat next to him. In the back window, a sign begged for understanding: "Italy. We are tourists. Sorry!!!"

▼

The zealousness of parking officers in one beach city gave rise to the bumper sticker: "Friends Don't Let Friends Park in Hermosa Beach."

▼

Hand-lettered sign on the back of a Jeep driven by a young woman in Manhattan Beach: "I'm new at this stick shift stuff—stay 10 feet behind."

▼

A minivan gliding along the Golden State Freeway bore this painted message above a large dent: "An accident no longer waiting to happen."

▼

The owner of a pickup truck had painted the words, "Present From My Wife," on the body of the vehicle. An arrow ran from the message to an unsightly dent.

▼

These two personalized license plates had a message for the San Diego Freeway: **HATE405** and **GDDM405**. But so did Deborah Moody of Van Nuys, whose plate cheerfully declared: **2JOY405**. "In L.A., we're about fun," she explained.

Honest advertising: A commercial for a used car dealer included this message: "Bankrupt? Bad credit? No money? No job? Come see us—when things get better."

seen on the freeway...

The motorcyclist with a laptop computer mounted to a gas tank. When traffic paused, he worked the keyboard.

▼

The young woman, clad in shorts, sunning herself on the hood of a car as it moved about 55 m.p.h. along the Harbor Freeway.

▼

The misdirected golf drive from a Westlake Village course that broke the windshield of a Thousand Oaks woman driving on the adjacent Ventura Freeway. The woman was uninjured.

▼

The motorist changing a flat on the shoulder of the Hollywood Freeway, only to have his spare tire roll across four lanes of traffic and come to a stop on the center divider.

▼

The man dressed as the devil and brandishing a 6-foot-long pitchfork at passing cars on the Santa Monica Freeway. He turned out to be an actor in a UCLA student film.

▼

Motorists practicing musical instruments as they maneuvered through traffic. Among the sightings: flute, trumpet, French horn and guitar.

▼

The disabled motorist who, while waiting for help, took out his clubs from the trunk and practiced his golf swing next to a guard rail.

Name changes: The Marina Freeway was renamed the Richard M. Nixon Freeway, but reverted to its original name after the Watergate scandal. The Century Freeway was renamed the Glenn M. Anderson Freeway in honor of a former lieutenant governor, but its original name remains in popular usage.

Presidential road report: After enduring the traffic in Moscow, former President Richard Nixon declared: "It's worse than the Santa Ana Freeway."

vanity plates that fail to please

A Culver City court reporter's personalized license plate was revoked because the letters — **TP U BG** — were keypad designations for the four-letter epithet known as the f-word.

The court reporter said she chose that message because **TP U BG** could also mean "if you can" in shorthand, a phrase from the children's story, "The Little Engine That Could."

The Department of Motor Vehicles rejected her explanation, and a four-year legal dispute ensued. Finally, a court settled the matter by ruling her intent "irrelevant" since there were more than 50,000 court reporters driving in California who couldn't take offense.

▼

Andrew Burg finally figured out why he was receiving parking tickets from California cities he hadn't visited. It was all because the license plate on his Honda said: **MISSING**. In each case, a police officer ticketing a motorist for driving without plates had written "Missing" in the space provided for the plate number. A computer dutifully matched each ticket with Burg's personalized plate.

▼

Another motorist, Robert Barbour, said he felt somewhat responsible for Burg's dilemma. His vanity plate read **NO PLATE**. Soon he was getting tickets from cities where officers had written "No Plate" on citations for plateless cars. The DMV then stepped in to help. Said Barbour: "They told me that they had advised officers to either write down the car's identification number or the word MISSING."

▼

Urban hiking writer John McKinney applied to the DMV for a personalized plate that said, **WALK LA**, only to have the agency ask for an explanation of its meaning. The DMV noted curtly that it had the right to refuse any combination of letters that might be "offensive to good taste and decency."

Maybe somebody should count the number of hours between 9 a.m. and 6 p.m.

when parking becomes a pain

Weekend parking places in Venice are often at a premium. So much so that one wily character in a parked car demanded $5 from a waiting driver before vacating the space.

▼

The two limousine drivers both wanted the same parking space at a supermarket in Redondo Beach. One brandished a BB gun that had been customized to look like a .45-caliber revolver. The other driver responded, "I'll show you a real weapon," and produced a loaded shotgun. Witnesses called police, who arrested the second driver.

▼

About those chalk marks: Two female motorists at a shopping plaza in upscale Palos Verdes Estates were arrested, handcuffed, frisked and jailed. Their alleged crime: trying to circumvent the one-hour parking limit by wiping off a meter maid's chalk marks. Meanwhile, in Beverly Hills an apparently disgruntled resident was spotted putting chalk marks on the tires of cars parked on Rexford Drive.

▼

An L.A. city report disclosed that 3,400 people had more than 20 unpaid parking tickets.

▼

Returning from one of his many trips abroad, Mayor Tom Bradley found there was no car waiting for him at LAX. It had been towed away after His Honor's chauffeur illegally parked it at the curb--in front of the Tom Bradley International Terminal.

▼

An actress on the "Seinfeld" TV show used the studio parking space assigned to actor/famous husband Tom Arnold. Later, she found obscenities scrawled on her car, as well as a photo of what appeared to be a large man's naked posterior.

An Upland man angry over a parking ticket tried to pay his fine with 2,000 pennies. But authorities exercised their legal right to refuse the box of coins. "We don't have time to stand here and count pennies," said one clerk.

▼

When fire erupted in the underground parking area of the Twin Towers office buildings in Century City, motorists were asked to exit to make room for fire equipment—only to be stopped by attendants demanding that they pay their toll first.

▼

The letter carried the imposing letterhead of "Baginda Sultanate of Sulu and North Borneo." The writer identified himself as honorary consul of same and said the city of L.A. should extend him diplomatic immunity in the matter of the enclosed parking ticket. Only one problem: the consulate hasn't existed since the late 1800s. "You have to admire the chutzpah of the guy," said a spokesman for the city attorney. The self-styled diplomat eventually paid up.

▼

David Spellerberg wanted to park his Rolls-Royce in front of his Beverly Hills art gallery each day. Problem was, the parking space had a one-hour meter. So Spellerberg told his chauffeur to feed the meter all day long, about $15 in change. But the city, declaring it was illegal to tie up a parking space that way, bombarded the Rolls with tickets. At one point, Spellerberg estimated he had received about 1,000 citations and paid $13,000 or so in fines. Finally, the city got a court order declaring the Rolls had to be moved after one hour. Spellerberg retaliated for a time by rotating a fleet of five Rolls in the same spot.

▼

The fine for parking on the sidewalk in L.A. ($30) is less than the fine for parking next to a red curb ($55).

miscelLAny

About 50,000 parking tickets were dismissed one year because of illegible handwriting by L.A. parking enforcement officers.

Sign in parking lot at L.A. County Museum of Art: **"Pre-pay in advance."**

meter maid memories

Raul Victorica felt fortunate when he spotted a parking meter with 30 minutes of time remaining. "But when I came back I had a ticket," he said. "And I still had 15 minutes more (on the meter)." On the ticket was the notation: "No Coins Deposited." Hard to believe, but it is a violation of the law to park in a metered space without "immediately depositing" coins. "You can't use prepaid space," said an L.A. parking official, who hastened to agree that it was "kind of a ticky-tack item."

▼

The world's toughest meter maids might be in the city of Paramount. Soon after the local Lions Club placed a wrecked automobile in a vacant lot with a sign reading "Don't Drink and Drive," the battered heap was ticketed. In a classic understatement, the meter maid checked a box on the citation that read, "Apparently inoperative." Paramount officials said the traffic officer didn't realize it was part of a city-approved safe-driving display for the holidays, and canceled the citation.

▼

Thrill-a-Minute L.A.: A downtown motorist parked his car after it was struck by a bullet and walked back a few blocks to try and spot the culprit. When he returned, he found a $55 parking ticket on his windshield.

It's simple: parking is prohibited three days per week, not to mention daily.

Downey, California, April 28,1992: The Rideshare prize
drawing was held today and the lucky rideshare participants
received the following:

LUIS R. VENTURA	GIFT CERTIFICATE FOR NURSERYLAND.
JOHNNITA FRAZIER	GIFT CERTIFICATE FOR NURSERYLAND.
JIMMY CAMACHO	GIFT CERTIFICATE FOR NURSERYLAND.
DONALD FINDLAY	GIFT CERTIFICATE FOR NURSERYLAND.
MANNY GONZALES	THE SOUGHT AFTER GAS CO. SWISS KNIFE.
JESUS ROBLES	GIFT CERTIFICATE FOR THE WHOREHOUSE.

They'll do anything to promote ride-sharing.

the madman started it all

Southern California was the birthplace of kooky automobile commercials, beginning with dealer Earl (Madman) Muntz, who dressed in Napoleonic hat and red long johns in the 1940s and shouted: "I want to give them away, but Mrs. Muntz won't let me. She's crazy!"

The Madman's showroom at 11th and Figueroa streets was a regular stop for tour buses and he was the frequent butt of jokes by comedians, especially Bob Hope. He died in 1987, but his name survived with the chain of electronics stores he founded.

Madman Muntz in 1951 with caricature of his old self.

There followed such offbeat TV car salesmen as Les Bacon ("Get off your couch and come on down to Hermosa Beach"), Chick Lambert with his dog Storm, Cal Worthington with his non-dogs named Spot, the fender-pounding Ralph Williams ("Hi, friends"), and Dick Lane ("Get on down to Central Chevrolet—I'll be there, will you?").

Lane, later a famous wrestling and roller derby announcer, was such a celebrity in the early days of the tube that literal-minded viewers would sometimes visit Central Chevrolet not to buy cars, but to see him.

Another TV pitchman, Frank Taylor, won favor among churchgoers because of his "No Sunday selling" slogan. But according to veteran public relations man Dick Tyler, "Frank Taylor's building and land were leased from a church, and his lease did not permit any business on Sunday. It was my first brush with, 'If you have a lemon, make lemonade.'"

streets of l.a.

Norma Jacobs wrote in the L.A. Conservancy News that when she was growing up in Southern California years ago, she was taught this ditty to find her way around downtown L.A.: "From *Main* you *Spring* to *Broadway*/Climb a *Hill* to *Olive*/Wouldn't it be *Grand* to *Hope*/To pick a *Flower* on *Figueroa*?"

You can't go west, young man.

City workers investigating a rash of stolen street signs said most of the losses were on streets with women's names. "We don't know if it's the boyfriends or what," said one. Hardest hit was Shirley Avenue in Tarzana.

Gen. Thaddeus Kosciuszko Way, a two-block-long downtown street named for a Polish-born hero of the Revolutionary War, is a tough name for L.A. police to handle. Retired Lt. Dan Cooke recalled the time that detectives tried to radio for assistance from Kosciuszko Way. "The location they gave sounded like 'Olivekosco,'" Cooke said. "They were asked to repeat it again and again...Finally, they just said, 'One block south of 1st Street.'"

At least it's only one block, either way.

DUELING SIGNS

Civic confusion.

Faith, Hope and Charity were once side-by-side streets in downtown L.A. But residents who resented jokes about "living on Charity" persuaded the city to rename their street Grand. Faith later became Flower. Hope remains.

▼

There actually was a Lover's Lane. Glen Creason, map librarian at L.A. Public Library, spotted it north of Union Station on an 1871 map. Later, the name was changed to Date Street for reasons unknown.

▼

Speedway, a Venice street, is so named because it was originally paved with bricks like the Indianapolis Speedway. A sports car race was held there early in the century.

▼

Michillinda Avenue in Pasadena was named by early settlers in honor of their home states of Michigan, Illinois and Indiana.

▼

In the old industrial section of L.A., Terminal Street is just a few blocks from Hemlock Street.

▼

You *can* end up on Easy Street. There's one in Highland Park and another in El Monte.

the day the traffic stopped

Midday traffic on the Ventura Freeway slowed to a crawl when motorists were startled by large message signs warning, "Gang War Riot Ahead" and "Killer Bee Gridlock." The signs turned out to be props for filming a "Brady Bunch" movie scene. But nobody had thought to warn drivers beforehand.

▼

A Northridge woman was locked in a traffic jam on the Golden State Freeway when she heard disc jockey Charlie Tuna declare her the winner of a drawing for several hundred dollars worth of stereo equipment. All she had to do to claim her prize was phone the station within 30 minutes. Alas, she couldn't get off the freeway in time.

▼

To promote car pooling, disc jockey Rick Dees broadcast his show from atop a Ventura Freeway overpass. But when Dees offered $100 to motorists if they could reach his mobile unit after hearing their cars described on the air, bedlam ensued on the pavement below. Some commuters unfurled banners and others stood through sun roofs and waved to attract Dees' attention. Winning drivers cut wildly across several lanes of traffic to collect their prizes. The result: A 15-mile backup of motorists whose drive time was increased by a half hour or more.

▼

Gridlocked on the Santa Monica Freeway on her way to work, talk show host/psychologist Barbara De Angelis did the first 25 minutes of her program over her car phone.

▼

Councilwoman Joy Picus, stalled in traffic on the Hollywood Freeway, was asked by a motorist in the next lane: "Would you mind calling my office and telling them I'm going to be late for the deposition?" The councilwoman cheerfully obliged.

Does He Come With a Warranty? In keeping with the campaign to call used cars "pre-owned cars," a dealership next to the Santa Ana Freeway posted a sign honoring an employee as PRE-OWNED MAN OF THE MONTH.

things that spill on the freeway:

Brassieres, a dead whale, thousands of dollars in coins and currency, sofas and chairs, carpeting, a refrigerator, a hot tub, bees, a load of L.A. Dodger programs, dozens of diapers, 864,000 cans of vegetables, a 200-pound pig (he survived), a load of catcher's masks, 27,000 pounds of almond shells, a boat and a surfboard. Not to mention the body that fell out of a coroner's van on the Hollywood Freeway.

just one of those days

A 2-year-old girl left with her 1-year-old brother in the family car shifted the gears into neutral, allowing the vehicle to roll across a four-lane street and into an apartment building in San Dimas. Their mother, 8½ months pregnant, gave chase. She then began suffering labor pains, and was rushed to the hospital. The pains turned out to be a false alarm. Amazingly, no one was injured.

Crews that stripe highway lanes have been known to paint over just about anything in their path — plants, hubcaps, trash and, in at least this case, road kill.

our honor roll of street signs

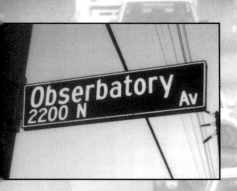

Obviously, the signmaker wasn't very observant.

An identity crisis for folks living on Friends Street.

This spelling job seems to have hit a new low.

Sign on eastbound Santa Monica Freeway told drivers the way to "Sacrafield." Meanwhile, on San Diego Freeway, a "Bakersmento" sign was sighted. The mixup was traced to a worker who reached into the wrong bin and grabbed a "field" suffix instead of a "mento" while putting up new signs.

At Santa Monica Freeway on-ramp, disagreement over required number of people for car-pool lane.

Stop and smell the what?

Passersby wondered how to pronounce this street name. Maybe "One Hundred Eleventy-First?" The tongue-twister eventually was replaced by a sign reading: "111th St."

Unlisted street in Sherman Oaks.

COURT ROOM

DIV. 30

the law

One of L.A.'s favorite gangsters, Mickey Cohen. See
page 97.

The steamroller as getaway car, and other **stupid criminal tricks**…The case of the giant **foam rubber breasts**…When lawyers upset judges (or, you'll never single-space in this town again)…Stories from the **not-exactly-a-crime file**.

When police seized a camcorder at the L.A. residence of a suspected burglar, they found a home movie inside. But the people in the video looked nothing like the suspect. So two TV stations volunteered to show excerpts of the video on news programs, figuring viewers might be able to identify the subjects. It worked. A Hawthorne couple who were the real owners of the camcorder phoned police. The cops arrested their suspect for possession of stolen goods. "He saw the program too," said Lt. Mike Melton, "so he wasn't completely surprised when we showed up."

▼

Glendale police, curious about the Humvee moving through the pre-dawn darkness with its headlights off, asked the driver how he came to possess the military vehicle. "President Clinton gave it to me," the man replied, adding: "You *do* know who the President is." Police arrested him anyway, figuring correctly that it was the Humvee reported missing by a National Guard unit.

▼

Jail officials were willing to dial the phone whenever their prisoner wanted to make a call. In fact, they insisted upon it. The prisoner was Kevin Mitnick, a Panorama City computer hacker. He wanted to be able to phone his family and his lawyer while awaiting trial in L.A. Prosecutors were skeptical, fearing that he had devised a way to access computers simply by dialing certain telephone numbers. But the 25-year-old computer whiz insisted on his rights. The solution: when Mitnick was ready to call family or lawyer, a guard punched in the numbers on a touch tone phone while Mitnick kept a safe distance, his handset attached to the end of a very long extension cord.

▼

When a Pomona Ford dealer left one of his new cars parked overnight with the key in the ignition, it seemed like an invitation to steal. And that's what it was. The problem, as three thieves discovered, was that this Ford had a few glitches, installed at the request of Pomona police. "We had been experiencing a lot of thefts at dealerships," Detective Ray Birch said. "So we got together with the dealer's mechanic and rigged up a little surprise for them." The thieves got only three blocks from the lot before the engine died and the power door locks jammed, imprisoning them in the car. "The arrests went very smoothly," Birch said.

▼

Salvador Ruiz went to the Firestone sheriff's station to report the theft of his carpet cleaning van, then stopped in a neighborhood church to say a prayer for its recovery. When he emerged, there was the van, parked nearby. Ruiz ran back to the station and alerted deputies, who seized the van and arrested its startled driver. Said Lt. Dennis Wilson of Ruiz: "He's a very religious man. He's probably more so now."

▼

A customer ended an argument with a Torrance gas station attendant by firing a gun into the air, then pointed the weapon at the attendant and drove off. The attendant grabbed a crowbar, jumped into his own car and gave chase. The customer, now alarmed, dialed 911 on his cellular phone and reported that "a crazy guy was chasing him," said Torrance Police Lt. Mike Tamble. The customer pulled into a sheriff's substation in Lomita — where he was arrested on suspicion of assault with a deadly weapon.

LOS ANGELES POLICE DEPARTMENT

DARYL F. GATES
Chief of Police

TOM BRADLEY
Mayor

P. O. Box 30158
Los Angeles, Calif. 90030
Telephone:
(213) 485-3202
Ref #:   1.1
FAX: 237-0676

May 11, 1992

Dear Mr. Kales:

I received your letter about me not wearing my seat belt while in
my car during the recent 60 Minutes program interviews. You are
absolutel right. During those times when I was being
interviewed, I was not wearing my seat belt.

Although I recognize that excuses are just that, excuses, I
believe your letter and expressed concern warrant an explanation.
First and foremost, I adamantly support the use of seat belts and
am meticulous about wearing them myself. Since Leslie Stahl and
the camera were both in the back seat, I turned around in my seat
and was nearly strangled by the three-point safety belt. My car
does not have a simple lap belt system, so I removed my seat
belt.

I hope that my decision to remove my seat belt for the interview
will not impact your decision to always wear your seat belt.
They do save lives, and I would hope you would choose to save
your own life by continuing to wear yours. As a final note,
although the camera did not show it, my aide was wearing, and
always wears, his seat belt. Stay safe.

Sincerely,

DARYL F. GATES
Chief of Police

*After an appearance on "60 Minutes" by Police Chief
Daryl F. Gates, Richard Kales of Santa Monica took Gates
to task for not wearing a seat belt as he rode through L.A.
with reporter Leslie Stahl. Gates wrote back that he was
guilty—but with an explanation.*

When a passing motorist threw a pomegranate that struck tow truck driver Michael Sherterkin on the 605 Freeway, the burly Sherterkin chased down his assailant's vehicle, hooked it up to his truck and towed it to a highway patrol office. Officers said the culprit's hands were still red.

▼

Two men walked up to an automatic teller machine in Southwest L.A. and fired 15 bullets into it, apparently hoping the ATM would spit out lots of money. Bad idea. Police who were staking out the area promptly arrested the pair.

▼

Burglary detectives watched as the two men in black rubber diving suits parked their car and disappeared into the darkness with an empty knapsack. They returned with knapsack bulging. Their booty? About 1,000 wet and slightly used golf balls fished out of a pond at the Van Nuys Golf Course. The two were arrested on suspicion of theft, but one detective admitted: "We thought we really had something a little more serious going on."

▼

West Hollywood sheriff's deputies knocked at the apartment door of a narcotics suspect and shouted their identification. From behind the closed door, a voice said: "Come in." But the door was locked, so they knocked again. "Come in," the voice repeated. But the door remained locked. Finally, search warrant and passkey in hand, the deputies let themselves in. While they were arresting a 34-year-old man on marijuana and cocaine charges, another deputy arrived and knocked at the door. "Come in," said a familiar voice from a small cage. It was the suspect's parrot.

▼

Diners in the elegant Tea Room of the Bullock's Wilshire Building were surprised to find white plastic spoons at their place settings. An apologetic waitress explained that several customers, aware that the landmark store was soon to close forever, had walked off with the silverware as souvenirs.

▼

If he didn't own two restaurants, Gerard Ferry never would have noticed the strange coincidence. Ferry received a letter at L'Orangerie from a man who claimed that a waiter had spilled a drink on him. A dry cleaning bill was enclosed, with a request that Ferry pay it. Then Ferry opened his mail at Pastel and found a letter that was identical —except that "Pastel" had been substituted for "L'Orangerie." When Ferry checked other upscale eateries, he found three that had received the same letter. Nobody paid up.

▼

Fans attending a UCLA-Washington football game at the Rose Bowl were asked to surrender their umbrellas before entering. Security precautions, apparently. The umbrellas could be picked up on the way out, spectators were told. Except that by game's end, they had all been stolen.

bugsy and mickey

Bugsy Siegel

Mickey Cohen and Bugsy Siegel were L.A.'s best known gangsters, and they both favored the same barbershop, Gornik-Drucker's in Beverly Hills. But Harry Drucker, its 88-year-old founder, became concerned when the rival hoodlums started coming into the shop at the same time.

"People were afraid they were going to pull out their guns and start shooting," manager Melody Pepaj recalled Drucker saying. Finally, Drucker asked Cohen not to come in any more.

On June 20, 1947, Siegel visited the shop for the last time. Later, freshly coiffed, he returned to his girlfriend's house, where he was shot to death by rival gangsters.

"The next day," Pepaj related, "Mickey Cohen called up and made a reservation."

take a bite, pay a penalty

The driver of a Commuter Express bus from downtown to Chatsworth suddenly stopped and declared: "I smell a cookie." He confiscated a bag of freshly baked goods from a passenger who had been nibbling on them in violation of bus rules. They were returned at the end of the ride.

▼

A downtown jewelry salesman was fined $104 after two undercover sheriff's officers caught him breaking Metro Rail's no-eating rule. He was observed popping candy into his mouth while riding the Blue Line.

YES	NO	VIOLATION(S)	DESCRIPTION(S)
☐	☐		
☐	☒	640(d)PC	EATING CHOCOLATE
☐	☐		COVERED CANDY ON TRAIN

The candy citation.

the old peel-down-to-your-underwear gambit

Burbank police looking for an escapee from Municipal Court on a cold winter morning chanced upon a swimmer in a nearby motel pool. The man helpfully pointed out the direction the escapee had taken. Upon closer inspection, police saw that the swimmer was clad in boxer shorts. He was transferred from the pool back to the cooler.

▼

Two men were arrested after they robbed a Silver Lake resident at knifepoint in his apartment, then stripped down to their underwear and donned bathrobes in an attempt to convince police that they lived there.

it takes a thief...

Less than two days after her family car was stolen, Julia Chang of Monterey Park got a call from police. The car had been recovered—with an anti-theft device called The Club still on the steering wheel. Funny thing, though. "We didn't own a Club," said Chang. "Apparently, the thieves didn't want our car stolen from them."

honor among thieves

It looked like a Blue Christmas for Victor Diaz of Sepulveda when thieves stole his van, which contained two six-packs of beer and toys for his four young children. The next morning Diaz spotted the car in Pacoima. The beer was gone—but the gifts were still there.

▼

Florence Savage of Studio City opened her front door one day to discover an envelope containing the wallet she had lost three years ago. A note, unsigned, read: "You dropped this wallet directly outside your car door on a side street off Ventura Blvd. I picked it up. I was broke and needed money. That is no excuse for stealing, I know. But I did it with the belief that I would return the wallet with the cash ($125) that was in it to you. It's taken much too long...but here it is."

▼

A woman locked her bicycle to a railing for safekeeping while she was away from her house. When she returned, the bike was gone. In its place was another bicycle—a rickety machine that obviously had seen better days. A bike owner trading up, apparently.

He deserves a special Emmy: After a convincing performance on the "America's Most Wanted" TV show, Santa Monica actor Christopher Cotten was spotted at a Nashville fair by two women who thought he was the fugitive he portrayed—David Adams, a Tennessee con man. They called police, who detained Cotten until the confusion was cleared up.

stupid criminal tricks

A motorist was infuriated by the ticket that the Santa Monica traffic officer had just left on his windshield. So he reached into the officer's vehicle, pulled its keys from the ignition, and then sped off in his own car. Police nabbed him and the keys the next day. A police sergeant explained the easy arrest: "We had his license plate number from the citation."

▼

Thieves broke into the car of Santa Monica shoe salesman Steve Katz and stole several bags filled with the latest designer styles from Europe. "They must have thought they were getting something great," said Katz's wife, Lauren. Only one problem: the shoes were all for the left foot.

▼

Three men in ski masks robbing a Rolling Hills Estates bank were in need of an empty bag for the money. So one of them emptied his bulging gym bag, and filled it with cash. Among the gym bag's contents left behind on the bank floor: two traffic tickets bearing the robber's name and address. It only got worse. When the hold-up men couldn't start their get-away car, they jumped into another and sped away. Left behind in the disabled car were wallets with identification for two of them. Police gathered up the telltale papers and quickly tracked down the trio.

▼

From the Gardena Valley News: A police officer encountered a man loitering near a bank. Without any urging, the man told the officer to "read him his rights because he was going to jail." When the officer expressed puzzlement, the suspect explained "that he was concealing a gun in his pants, and that it was falling down the pants leg."

Another White House gang: When two members of L.A. street gangs were invited to President Clinton's inauguration, some police were offended. At LAPD's Newton Station, this fictitious entry was added to a list of gangs in the area: "Clinton Gangster Crips."

A cop story: An incident at The Short Stop, a Sunset Boulevard bar long known as a cop hangout, inspired this anecdote in a Joe Wambaugh novel, "Fugitive Nights": A would-be robber enters the bar. He appears to be holding a gun under his coat. The intruder doesn't realize that half the rumpled guys hunched over drinks are plainclothes cops. One of them shoots him to death. Afterwards, it is discovered that the dead man was holding a comb, not a gun. Hence the bar's new bumper sticker: "Use a Comb, Go to Heaven."

An East Los Angeles man stole a steamroller and led police officers on a low-speed chase for a few blocks before surrendering. He said he took the steamroller because he was tired of walking.

▼

Star News, an L.A. County Sheriff's Department publication, reported this judicial drama: A robbery victim was asked, "Are the men who robbed you present in the courtroom today?" Before the victim could respond, both defendants raised their hands.

▼

A crime log reported juveniles **"throwing rocks and homes and cars."**

Three robbers impatient with the response from workers at a Santa Monica fast-food restaurant jumped behind the counter. They grabbed what they thought was the cash register and took off. Actually, it was an adding machine. Noted one officer: "They weren't real pros."

▼

'Twas the 27th day before Christmas, and in the Los Felix Market a creature was stirring in the building's chimney. A store employee hearing the disturbance phoned sheriff's deputies, who discovered a would-be burglar stuck with his hands above his head. Firemen freed him with a rope so he could be taken into custody.

▼

A drunk driver ended a 14-minute pursuit by pulling into the parking lot of the downtown city jail. He told officers he had been arrested before and "knew where to go."

▼

"Happiness Is Being a Grandparent," said the license plate frame on a Chevrolet spotted by Long Beach police. Odd thing was that the passengers were six youths—between the ages of 13 and 17, as it turned out. After pulling them over, police discovered that the car had been stolen.

Hollywood artist John Thompson heard it on his police scanner: "The dispatcher said a fellow walked into a hardware store in Hollywood and was trying to talk the employees into sawing off his handcuffs. He apparently had escaped from a near-by location. About five minutes later, the dispatcher reported the man was back in custody."

are you sure this is a good idea?

A 49-year-old L.A. man was chased and captured by two LAPD officers after stealing an American flag and a DARE banner from the flagpole in front of a 6th Street building—the LAPD's Central Division.

▼

L.A. County Sheriff Sherman Block was once a counterman at Canter's Delicatessen on Fairfax Avenue.

Police arrested a man for digging up sections of lawn and placing them in a shopping cart, apparently intending to plant the turf elsewhere. He might have gotten away with it except that the grass he removed was part of the lawn at LAPD's Wilshire Division station.

▼

A sneak thief grabbed two dozen T-shirts from a table on the steps of City Hall and took off running. Five men quickly chased him down. "He was astonished to find out they were off-duty police officers," said a witness. The culprit must not have noticed that the T-shirts bore a photo of Chief Daryl Gates and the words, "Citizens in Support of the Chief of Police."

▼

During a sting operation, two men in Lennox tried to buy cocaine from a sheriff's deputy whose jacket said "Sheriff" and whose cap bore the word "Narcotics" and the letters "LASD."

When more than your attitude needs adjusting.

After Hours Chiropractic   Open 'til 10 p.m.

EDWARDS

from the
not-exactly-a-crime file

A bus driver on Ventura Boulevard called an MTA dispatcher to report a passenger with a "Colt .45" in his waistband. Police boarded the bus and, sure enough, found a guy with a quart of Colt 45 malt liquor tucked in his pants.

▼

A package left at a Century City office building bore the words, "This is a bomb threat." The LAPD bomb squad blew it up with explosives, then made a surprising discovery: the package had contained a movie script. The sender, an unidentified screenwriter, said he only wanted to draw attention to his story about a "human bomb." He was not charged.

▼

Photographer Henk Friezer heard this tale from an L.A. cop. During a rainstorm, a man was driving down an Eagle Rock street with his head protruding from the car window. It seemed like odd behavior in a rainstorm, so the cop pulled him over. The explanation was simple. The driver had just bought several bags of fertilizer at K Mart and couldn't stand the fumes.

Deputies at the Santa Clarita Valley sheriff's station rushed to a billboard in Saugus after callers reported a body hanging from the structure. What they found was a mannequin hanging by its fingers—part of an advertisement for chiropractor David Reuben.

miscelLAny

The Downey police department prohibited more than two officers from gathering at the same doughnut shop at the same time.

Police rushed to a Chatsworth elementary school where a man wearing Army fatigues and carrying a rifle was reportedly parked across the street. He turned out to be a guest speaker who had brought along a Civil War-era rifle and costume.

▼

When men in frontier garb staged a mock holdup of an Agoura Hills bank to promote a Pony Express Days festival, an alarmed onlooker rushed to call sheriff's deputies. Four patrol cars responded, adding an extra touch of realism.

▼

It was not the usual freeway-leaper bulletin: "We got a call that a man in an angel outfit with wings was on the overpass," said a CHP officer. "People thought he was going to jump." Officers hurried to the Santa Ana Freeway location only to find out that the man was a character in a movie.

▼

LAPD dispatchers sent out this bulletin: "At Wilshire and Wilton, a 187 (murder) victim." About five minutes later, patrol officers responded: "Code 4 (no further assistance needed). It's a mannequin."

▼

A car on the San Diego Freeway was pulled over by a cop who was suspicious about the long, pipe-like object in the driver's mouth. The cop let the motorist go after seeing that the object came with a booklet entitled, "How to Play the Kazoo."

▼

Several suspicious residents told police they had seen "a man wearing a mask in a car," the South Pasadena Review reported. Police tracked down the suspect, who turned out to be a large dog.

Married attorneys need not apply.

court report

Deputy Dist. Atty. Ed Kosmal, ticketed in Beverly Hills for walking his dog without a leash, pleaded not guilty on grounds that he controlled the animal with a "psychological leash." He called the dog as a witness to prove his point, but the judge found Kosmal guilty anyway. A fine was suspended when the defendant promised to switch to a physical leash.

▼

A North Hollywood man arrested for drunk driving said he didn't know that someone had put vodka in the Jell-O he ate for dessert. A jury rejected his defense after prosecutors noted that he had had three helpings.

▼

California Lawyer magazine reported the case of an L.A. homeless man who served 10 days of a friend's jail term "because he had nothing better to do." The substitute inmate fooled court officials by showing up and announcing: "I'm here to start my sentence."

Dear Jim And Gordon,

Just A Brief Note to wish you Both A Wonderful Holiday Season. You guys truely Are the Best at what you do. I wouldn't of wanted Anyone else up there making me look sooooo BAD. I Am really sorry for All the trouble I've caused you And your staff, But the real tragedy would of Been if I Haven't Learned Anything through All of this. But I HAVE! God Bless you Both And I wish you All the Best in the future.

All My Best wishes,

Barry

REMEMBERING YOU
is ONE of THE special joys
of THE SEASON.

Barry Minkow, the youthful carpet-cleaning whiz convicted of 57 counts of fraud, sent a Christmas card to his prosecutors, with a note praising them as "the best at what you do."

Small-claims court somehow seemed the wrong forum for a dispute involving size 99 MMM foam rubber breasts. A Chatsworth adult-video company had ordered the giant falsies from a Buena Park special-effects firm. But when they arrived, they were deemed too large and wrinkly. The filmmakers demanded the return of a $2,500 payment, but the creators of the bogus breasts called them "beautiful" and said the stretch marks made them "look realistic." A Van Nuys judge ruled against the video company, then commented sourly: "I want to tell you how appalled I am by the business you are in and my disdain that you are taking up the court's time with this matter."

Cynthia Albritton, once known as Cynthia Plaster Caster for her anatomically accurate reproductions of the private parts of rock musicians, won $10,000 in damages from a music publisher. The latter had refused to return 23 of her works because of a business dispute with Albritton. Among her subjects: the late rock guitarist Jimi Hendrix.

▼

Two Encino attorneys who were neighbors gained national notoriety when one sued the other over noise from backyard basketball games. The dispute bounced in and out of court for years. At one point, a lower court restricted the ballplaying to a six-hour period. But an appellate court vacated the order, and suggested that the complaining neighbor try closing windows to restore quiet.

▼

Danny Gomez, age 3, ticketed for running a stop sign and driving without a license or insurance, managed to beat the rap in a San Pedro court. A judge threw out the case after it was determined that someone joyriding in his mother's car had identified himself as Danny Gomez and given officers the Gomez family address.

▼

A traffic court study by USC researchers turned up these alibis from L.A. drivers protesting their tickets:

"I was driving a new Mercedes that was shipped from Europe. It doesn't show your speed in m.p.h.; it shows it in kilometers."

"I was asking directions from a woman at the bus stop and had no idea she was a prostitute. I was not on the sidewalk (but) had pulled into the gas station."

"I left my curling iron on, and was rushing to get home to turn it off before the house burned down."

The judge's verdicts on all three: Hah. Hah. Hah.

▼

City Wok, a Chinese restaurant in the San Fernando Valley, filed suit to prohibit MCA from using "CityWalk" as the name of its new entertainment complex in Universal City. Otherwise, said the restaurant, its customers might become confused. The dispute was settled out of court.

my life as a juror

The Santa Monica judge asked if any of the prospective jurors felt they should be excused. One man raised his hand and told the judge, "Your honor, I cannot be on this panel because the prosecuting attorney looks exactly like my ex-wife." Excused.

▼

Among the instructions given to a group of jury candidates in the Long Beach courthouse was this warning: "Don't throw paper planes off the balcony."

▼

A prospective juror being questioned by Superior Court Judge J. Stephen Czuleger mentioned that he had once been inside a Winchell's doughnut shop when it was robbed. Asked if he was satisfied with the police response, the man paused before saying, "Yes." When the judge asked him to explain his hesitation, the man replied: "Usually, there's an officer in a doughnut shop and there was none there at the time."

▼

Of the 2.1 million residents sent jury-service questionnaires in L.A. County one year, one third did not respond.

it's the law

If you're a resident of Paramount, city law permits you to hold just one garage sale per lot per year—unless you die. Then your family is allowed to hold an extra sale to get rid of your things.

▼

In 1965, the L.A. City Council, angered by Venice's beatniks, outlawed the nighttime playing of bongo drums at the beach.

▼

The Downey City Council outlawed golf-playing at graveyards after getting complaints that trespassing duffers were disturbing the tranquility of the Downey Cemetery.

▼

The Monrovia City Council approved an ordinance to ban disrobing, bathing and shaving in public restrooms. Still permitted: washing face and hands as well as arms—but only up to the elbows. Complaints about street people led to the ban.

A police report on an unusual distress case.

109

briefly put, don't upset the judge

A Superior Court judge fined Spray Gould & Bowers $2,500 because the typewritten lines in one of the law firm's filings were one-and-a-half spaced instead of double-spaced. An appeals court later vacated the fine.

▼

After submitting a brief in federal court, a Manhattan Beach attorney was ordered before a judge to explain why he had used a type font that yielded 15 characters per inch rather than 10. The judge suspected he was trying to evade a 35-page limit. The attorney said he thought the font was "more aesthetically pleasing." He was let off with a warning.

▼

Another L.A. judge fined a lawyer $1,500 because he filed too much paperwork. The judge had told the lawyer to keep a memorandum to no more than seven pages. The lawyer did so, but angered the judge by tacking on a 1,500-page appendix. The fine was overturned on appeal.

They should have called a lawyer: Five candidates at a state Bar exam in Pasadena stopped what they were doing and rushed to assist a fellow test-taker who was suffering an epileptic seizure. When they returned to the test, their examiners refused to give them extra time to compensate for the interruption. But critical public reaction forced the Bar to retreat. It gave all five certificates of appreciation and adjusted their marks "for lost time."

in search of lawyerly good deeds

The Beverly Hills Today newspaper had a nice idea—a series entitled "Great Deeds by the Attorneys." In a note to readers, the paper said: "We would be most grateful to receive any good news about good things the lawyers have done, and we promise to print them in this new column." Days passed. No lawyerly good deeds were reported. The newspaper then ran a blank box to dramatize its plea.Finally, the paper received—and published—its first submission, copy editor Chris Sharp said. No need for L.A. barristers to feel smug, though. "It's about a lawyer in Orange County," Sharp said.

what about serenading babies?

Some old-time laws on L.A.'s books in the 1800s and early 1900s:

- No serenading women without a license.
- Pickles may not be manufactured downtown.
- No snuff may be given to a child under 16.
- Bathing two babies in a single bathtub at one time is forbidden.
- Every citizen shall sweep in front of his house on Saturdays.
- Shops and taverns to close in winter at 8 p.m., in summer at 9 p.m.
- No one shall walk the streets "in a scandalous attire or molest the neighbors with yells."

He already gave.

the O.J. papers

My name is Marcia and I'll be your prosecutor:

A newsletter from Lawry's The Prime Rib displayed a photo of prosecutor Marcia Clark in the mid-'70s when she was a waitress at the La Cienega eatery. There was also a separate photo of O.J. Simpson visiting the restaurant. "O.J. dined frequently in our Beverly Hills restaurant," the newsletter confided, "but we haven't been able to discover whether Marcia was ever his waitress."

Some motorists used their vanity license plates to comment on the O.J. Simpson case. There was the 1994 white Ford Bronco with the plate, **NOT OJS**. Car and Driver magazine turned up a plate that said: **OJDIDIT**. Also seen locally: **IM40J**, **ASKKATO** and **THE DNA**. Presiding over it all was **ITOAUTO**—on a tow truck.

After learning that the city of L.A. was looking for a new slogan, the always helpful David Letterman submitted: "L.A.: Come Sequester Yourself!"

And would it be admissible in court? A marquee in front of a West L.A. church asked: "What Would Jesus Say to O.J.?"

A personal ad placed by an unidentified woman sought a "blond, tan Kato Kaelin type."

Roulette players at the Flamingo Hilton in Las Vegas were observed putting their chips on No. 32 — Simpson's football jersey number at USC — and chanting, "O.J.! O.J.!" as the wheel spun.

That's one way of looking at it: A Lexus dealer in Minnesota sent out this service reminder after O.J. Simpson's arrest:

"Mrs. Joelson, The last time we saw you, O.J. was a free man. Since then, he's received much more attention than your car. The last service on your ES250 was on March 14, 1994. Please call for an appt."

Hermosa Beach bar promised refuge for those who had seen enough of the trial.

"I am sick of the case," said mail clerk Cindy Moody, and for good reason. Her post office in Brentwood—not the L.A. suburb that Simpson called home, but a small town east of San Francisco—received as many as 500 pieces of mail a day intended for the defendant. The mail included fruit baskets and at least one knife catalog.

Before the trial began, Crown Book outlets sequestered copies of Faye Resnick's lurid memoir of Nicole Brown Simpson behind placards that said: "Attention Potential O.J. Simpson Jurors. We Will Be Happy to Hold Your Book Until After the Trial."

The black plaintiff in a suit against a Northern California water district claimed he lost his case because at one point the judge referred to him as Mr. Simpson, causing the jury to laugh.

Virtual reality: CNN producer Laura Ornest, dining in a Beverly Hills restaurant, noticed Simpson attorney Robert Shapiro at a nearby table. So did her waiter, Paul Witten, who said, "I wish I were waiting on him." Explained Witten: "I play Ron Goldman in the movie." (Fox's "O.J. Simpson Story.")

Rolling out a tribute to the Simpson trial cast.

*Maybe term limits is a
more reasonable approach.*

politics

L.A. and the Presidency (learn which former President once sold drill bits here)…The dead candidate who won the election anyhow…**Sonny Bono** articulates on articulation…Notes from the campaign trail…**Our Watergate grads.**

An L.A.-type surprise greeted members of the press covering the Michael Dukakis campaign in 1988. The reporters had been given red and blue bandanas during a Texas stopover. But when the campaign came to Southern California later in the day, Secret Service agents asked them to stash the bandanas. The colors, the agents cautioned, were the same worn by members of the Bloods and Crips gangs to identify themselves.

▼

Bill Walleck of Bent Parade Floats recalled this scene at the 1973 Rose Parade: then-First Lady Pat Nixon riding in a convertible, followed by the USC Trojan marching band. Nothing unusual, except that the costumed band members with instruments in the front row were actually Secret Service agents.

▼

While Gov. Pete Wilson was on the campaign trail, several of the big Caltrans traffic signs on Southland freeways flashed a surprising endorsement: "PETE WILSON FOR PRESIDENT." The bogus messages were an apparent attempt to embarrass Wilson in retaliation for Caltrans layoffs.

▼

Don't mess with L.A. drivers: As President Bush's motorcade cruised along La Cienega Boulevard in rush-hour traffic, motorists in its path

miscelLAny

A convicted murderer named Dave Brown, about to be hanged near L.A. City Hall in 1854, reportedly said he would meet his Maker with a clear conscience because "I can at least claim that I was never either mayor or member of the Los Angeles City Council."

Stephen Foster, mayor of L.A. from 1854-56, solidified his law-and-order credentials by resigning from office to help lynch a convicted killer whose execution had been stayed by the state Supreme Court.

The house number at Ronald and Nancy Reagan's Bel-Air residence was changed from 666 to 668, reportedly because Mrs. Reagan was troubled that the original number represented Satan in the Bible.

were ordered over to the side. One exasperated driver rolled down his window and gave a one-fingered salute. So did the next motorist, and the next and the next and the next. Bush missed the salutes, however. As he passed by, he appeared to be engrossed in a newspaper.

ten facts about l.a. and the white house

1. Number of local voters supporting **Abraham Lincoln** in the election of 1860: 179, placing him third in the returns.

2. First President to visit L.A.: **Rutherford B. Hayes**, 1880. The City Council allocated $25 for a banquet in his honor.

3. Only First Lady to die in L.A. County: **Lucretia R. Garfield**, in South Pasadena, 1918 – 37 years after her husband's assassination.

4. Future President who worked as a law clerk in San Bernardino: **Lyndon Johnson**, 1925.

5. Cities in which **George Bush** lived while working as a drill-bit salesman in the 1940s: Huntington Park, Whittier, Compton and Ventura.

6. Nominated for President at the L.A. Sports Arena: **John F. Kennedy**.

7. Candidate who told Jerry Brown during 1992 campaign to "Chill out, you're from California.": **Bill Clinton**.

8. First Ladies who lived in Whittier: **Lou Hoover, Nancy Reagan** and **Barbara Bush**.

9. Most memorable line by a future President: "You won't have **Nixon** to kick around anymore because, gentlemen, this is my last press conference." In the Beverly Hilton Hotel, Nov. 7, 1962, following Nixon's defeat in the California gubernatorial election.

10. Number of streets in Monterey Park named after obscure Presidents: 8 (**Polk** Way; **Harrison** Road; **Buchanan** and **Pierce** Places; **Van Buren, Tyler, Taylor** and **Fillmore** Drives).

watergate u

Local universities were well represented in the Nixon Administration during the Watergate scandal:

USC alumni – **Dwight Chapin, Ronald Ziegler, Gordan Strachan** and **Donald Segretti.**

UCLA alumni – **H.R. Haldeman** (who also attended USC and Redlands), **John Ehrlichman** and **Alexander Butterfield.**

Whittier College alumni – **Richard M. Nixon.**

on the campaign trail

Please don't feed the candidates: Mike Woo, campaigning for mayor, was late for an appearance at the Blue Line terminal. A frazzled aide who was waiting there barked into a two-way radio to Woo's driver: "I want him here right now. We'll feed and water him later."

▼

Sonny Bono, admitting that he was less articulate than some other candidates: "If I could be like these guys, I would love it. But, you know, that's something I guess I'm gonna have to learn, how to throw that articulation out there."

▼

Can we draft him for President? A sign in a Beverly Hills gas station read: "Re-elect Bernie Hecht, Beverly Hills City Council. Vision. Integrity. Shorter Speeches."

▼

Curtis Tucker (D-Inglewood) won an Assembly election in 1988 — one month after he died. He received 71% of the vote. "The people have made it clear they wish to be represented by a Democrat, no matter what the circumstances," said his disappointed opponent.

A hill is a hale is a hillhale: During the 1992 campaign, write-in candidates in California were invited to provide alternate spellings of their names so election officials could better interpret what voters wrote on their ballots. Lois Hill Hale, a state Senate candidate from Inglewood, submitted more than 20 variations, including:

Lois Hail Hill
Lois Hill Hall
Lois Hillhale
Lola Hill Hale
Louis Hill Hale
Lewis Hill Hale
Dr. Hill-Hale
Loyce Hill
Luis Hill
Ms. Holl

Don't mess with Maverick: Images of Hollywood swirled around a 1980 ballot dispute in Huntington Beach. City Council candidate Jack Kelly asked to be listed as "businessman/actor (Maverick)" in sly recognition that he once co-starred in the cowboy television series of that name. An opponent, John Valentino, then threatened to list himself as John (Rudolph) Valentino. Maverick made the ballot; Rudolph didn't. Kelly was elected.

FOLLOW THESE SIMPLE DIRECTIONS

It would be difficult to cast there, anyway.

A door with a nasty temper.

VETERANS' BENEFITS
VERIFICATION AND REFERRAL

NOTE: DO NOT COMPLETE THIS FORM UNLESS ONE OF THE
FOLLOWING IS KNOWN: VETERAN'S SOCIAL SECURITY NO
AND DATE OF BIRTH. MILITARY SERIAL NO., OR VETERANS
ADMINISTRATION (V.A.) CLAIM NO.

This is a mail referral only.
Do not send the Veteran.

Don't Fed-Ex them, either.

Making sure everyone has enough personal space.

We thought it was more like 12%.

Whatever you say.

Not usually required when doing the laundry.

Wonder what it says on the elevator.

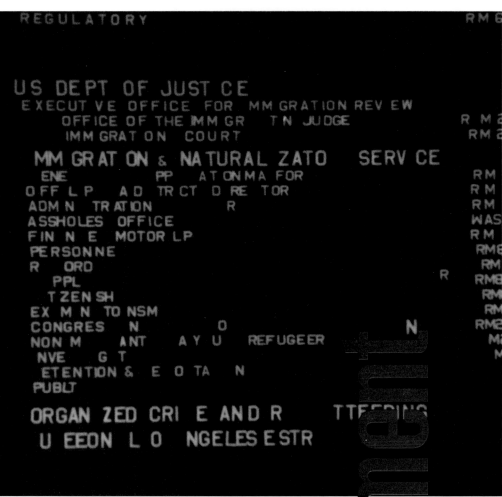

US DEPT OF JUST CE
EXECUT VE OFFICE FOR MM GRATION REV EW
OFFICE OF THE IMM GR T N JU DGE   R M 2
IMM GRAT ON COURT   RM 2

MM GRAT ON & NATURAL ZATO SERV CE
ENE PP AT ON MA FOR   RM
OFF L P AD TR CT D RE TOR   R M
ADM N TR AT ION R   R M
ASSHOLES OFFICE   WAS
FIN N E MOTOR LP   R M
PERSON NE   RM 8
R ORD   R RM
PPL   RM 8
T ZEN SH   RM
EX M N TO NSM   RM
CONGRES N O   N RM 8
NON M ANT A Y U REFUGEE R   M 2
NVE G T   M
ETENTION & E O TA N
PUBL T

ORGAN ZED CRI E AND R TT FFING
U EE ON L O NGELES E STR

In downtown Federal Building, one eyebrow-raising entry stood out among the mysteriously jumbled letters in lobby directory.

government

The DWP's better ideas (like bottled water for its offices)...Flying chairs, fistfights and other **civic disturbances**...Irwindale's **Hungarian flag salute** to Mexican independence... Keeping our school children safe from the dreaded backward R.

A 1991 study identified 1,200 forgotten motions still pending before the L.A. City Council, dozens of them more than 10 years old and some of them proposed by since-deceased council members.

▼

A plan to make the L.A. County children's court in Monterey Park "child sensitive" ran into trouble when it was disclosed that judges would sit on platforms elevated only 6 inches above the floor. While that might be less intimidating than the standard 18-inch elevation, officials said it offended "the dignity of the court." They compromised at 12 inches.

▼

Some 75 beauticians and barbers were invited to meet with the Santa Clarita City Council, which asked them what people in town were talking about. "Everyone talks to their hairdresser," one city official explained. Among the disclosures at the unusual session: the city needs more recreational facilities. Said one manicurist: "You can only bowl so much."

▼

Culver City school officials rejected "Little Red Riding Hood" because the book depicts Red taking Grandma a bottle of wine to pep her up.

When the Sons of Italy erected a statue of Christopher Columbus at the county government mall, they had to settle for a pint-sized tribute. They were instructed to make the statue shorter than a nearby sculpture of George Washington, apparently to avoid offending the general's admirers.

▼

Walt Disney originally wanted to put Mickey Mouse Park (as he first called Disneyland) in Burbank. But there was opposition from the City Council, including one member who said: "We don't want the carny atmosphere in Burbank."

▼

The Long Beach Unified School District advised students not to wear Natas clothing because the name "spelled backwards is Satan." The notice was rescinded after school officials learned that Natas was the first name of a famous skateboarder.

▼

The RTD board of directors, noting that the $42 cost of a monthly bus/rail pass was "a hardship" for some riders, agreed to offer a two-week pass for $23. Or you could buy two for $46 and ride an entire month.

▼

Cerritos once forbade a Toys R Us store from displaying the trademark backward "R" in its logo because the city feared it would confuse impressionable schoolchildren. Eventually, the city reversed itself.

▼

An agricultural inspector in Torrance dutifully placed a Medfly trap on a tree which was barren except for plastic fruits and vegetables placed there as a joke.

122

El Monte Union High School District

3537 Johnson Avenue • El Monte, California 91731
(818) 444-9005 FAX (818) 448-8419

Dear Mr. DiConti;

Your vision and life will terminate as of September 30, 1994; as well as your dental, however, if you wish, you may continue your dental coverage for 18 months. A cost sheet and Cobra papers are

Mr. DiConti was looking forward to a long, healthy retirement until he got this note.

In a directive from the mayor's office banning sexist words from reports, L.A. city officials were advised to use the phrase "maintenance hole covers" instead of "manhole covers."

▼

A Pasadena woman received a letter of commendation from the city because her water usage had dropped 25% in the past year. The note asked permission to publish her photograph in the Pasadena Star-News, along with a story telling how she managed such a reduction. She declined. "I doubt they'd want to print my reason," she said. "It decreased because I got a divorce."

▼

When a librarian at the Southwestern University Law School wrote to the L.A. city clerk's office requesting a list of City Council members, he instead received a sheet with the betting spreads for that week's pro football games.

▼

Hungarian flags were hung in front of the Irwindale City Hall during fiesta days honoring Mexico's independence. A city official defended the odd tribute by noting that the flags of the two countries had the same colors, and besides, "They're just festival flags."

Oops! Santa Monica Mayor Dennis Zane kicked off an environmental awareness campaign by saying: "We have many things to celebrate today, not the least of which is the venereal equinox."

Most confusing public inscription: "A people cannot have the consciousness of being self-governed unless they attend themselves to things over against their own doors." Carved on the Main Street side of City Hall.

L.A. County's 400 air-raid warning sirens were unplugged in 1985 after it was discovered that a third of the devices were broken. Many of the silent sirens were left in place, however, because it was judged too costly to remove them.

Memorial to Robert Citron, the disgraced ex-treasurer of Orange County? Nope. An intersection in Pomona.

When a Pasadena nurse applied for unemployment insurance, the state mailed a letter to her last employer. The employer was asked to verify the nurse's stated reason for leaving her job. The state got no response, which should not have been a surprise. As the nurse had noted on her application form, her reason for leaving the job was: "EMPLOYER DIED."

▼

Every city should have its own foreign policy: In 1980, ignoring the U.S. government's decision to recognize Communist China and sever diplomatic relations with Taiwan, the L.A. City Council ordered the flag of Taiwan raised over City Hall.

▼

The Redondo Beach City Council once voted to adopt the Goodyear Blimp as the city's official bird, though the creature's nest is really in neighboring Carson.

▼

State Sen. Charles Calderon (D-Whittier), who sponsored a bill giving women the right to wear pants at work, explained that he had "worn a skirt on occasion—during Halloween or pranks—(and) it's the most uncomfortable thing I've ever worn."

▼

You might think that Beacon H. Pedro would be nervous after receiving a letter from the state Franchise Tax Board that said: "We have reviewed our files of 1991 California personal income tax returns. Our files do not show you filed a return."

But Beacon H. Pedro wasn't worried because there was no such person. The letter was sent to the Beacon House Assn. of San Pedro, an organization for recovering alcoholics. "Somehow, they mistook our tax-exempt registration number for a Social Security number," said a Beacon House spokesman.

Taking a tough stand on sick days.

civic disturbances

The dialog between L.A. County Supervisors Pete Schabarum and Deane Dana sometimes baffled onlookers. One day, Schabarum grew angry at Dana for switching his position on an issue, and growled:

"Some guy calls you up this morning and says, 'Holy cow, dabba dabba dabba doo…'"

To which Dana had this nifty response: "Some people call up you and dabba dabba doo."

▼

Bell Gardens Mayor Josefina Macias, angered by what she considered sexist comments, attempted to slap Councilman Frank Duran and then threw a chair at him. Afterwards, Duran said: "You know how women are."

▼

After Hawaiian Gardens City Councilwomen Lennie Wagner and Kathleen Navejas duked it out, each claimed to be the victim. Navejas said she was kicked by Wagner; Wagner said she was punched by Navejas. Each said the other spilled coffee on her.

▼

The Azusa City Council banned Mayor Eugene Moses from opening the refrigerator at City Hall after grumblings that he had snatched some employees' food.

Why bother? "L.A. Convention Center" was the winning entry in a contest to rename the facility. Its old name: L.A. Convention and Exhibition Center.

City council members in Lawndale used a button and light system to signal their desire to speak during a meeting. When her button repeatedly failed, an exasperated Councilwoman Carol Norman began blowing shrill blasts on a whistle to get attention. "Here comes the Barnum & Bailey Circus again," growled a colleague as she sounded off. Norman escalated her campaign by appearing next in a red firefighter's hat with a revolving red light on top. The council responded by banning whistles and flashing lights. And Norman's button was finally fixed.

▼

They can't blame this one on Ollie North: A delinquent tax list issued by Ventura County in 1994 included the following entry: "The Ronald Reagan Presidential Foundation, 40 Presidential Drive, $1,124.26."

Diamond Bar City Councilman Clair Harmony was accused of body-slamming Councilwoman Phyllis Papen and provoking fistfights with Councilmen Gary Werner and Gary Miller. Harmony said the complaints were an attempt to discredit his anti-corruption campaign—and besides, he was only trying to defend himself.

meanwhile, at the dwp...

After a $500,000 advertising campaign to persuade residents to drink water from their taps, the L.A. Department of Water and Power admitted that seven of its offices furnished bottled water to employees.

▼

• Consideration of inserting information in the next city sewer about the state's budget crisis and its impact locally.

A clue to how the city council in Thousand Oaks feels about the state's budget crisis.

Because the agency was $3.40 short on the postage for its property tax bill, it was ordered to pay $333,407 in late penalties.

▼

After the DWP provided energy-efficient light bulbs to its customers as part of "A Better Idea," the agency notified 10,000 residents from Hollywood to South L.A. that one brand could pose a safety hazard. DWP workers had to go house to house to recall the bulbs.

ingenuity in government

The county Road Department lined Jefferson Boulevard in Marina del Rey with 900 artificial palms and other plants after deciding there was not enough earth along the roadway to support real plants.

Environmental terrorists tore out 50 of the ersatz greenery and the county removed the rest after criticism from garden clubs and others.

▼

After a hiring freeze was imposed at City Hall, employees of the Personnel Department were asked to suggest a snappy phrase to replace the department's old slogan, "We Have a Job for You!"

▼

Spectators climbing into trees during sports celebrations on the City Hall lawn sometimes lost their footing and fell.

That prompted the city to paint numbers on 32 of the trees so that paramedics could be directed to a specific tree if someone took a tumble.

"The spotters can say, 'Go to tree so-and-so and rescue someone,'" a spokesman explained.

THE CITY OF LOS ANGELES
OFFERS
COMPETITIVE PROMOTION

MECHANICAL REPAIR SUPERVISOR
(Code No. 3795)

THE SALARY for Mechanical Repair Supervisor is flat-rated at $3967 a month. In some positions, higher salaries are paid for obnoxious work.

And what might that be?

distinctly

IT'S HARD TO SPOT THE FAKES IN THIS TOWN

(advertisement for gas logs)

JUST WHAT L.A. NEEDS—MORE HEELS!

(shoe company)

WE ALL ARRIVED IN LOS ANGELES AS TRANSPLANTS. HOW ABOUT LEAVING AS ONE?

(organ-donor campaign)

A bootmaker's dig at Hollywood.　　　*How to communicate with the jocks in L.A.*

MEETINGS ARE LIKE RELATIONSHIPS. SOMETIMES YOU NEED MORE SPACE.

(L.A. Convention Center)

MORE HAIR-RAISING RIDES THAN THE RTD

(Hollywood Park race track)

**FROM EL SEGUNDO, YOU HAVE A PERFECTLY CLEAR VIEW
OF THE SMOG THAT HANGS OVER L.A.**

(promoting city of El Segundo)

YOU CAN'T DO THIS WITH JUST ANY CAMCORDER

(black-and-white police car visible through viewfinder)

DON'T GO TO BED 'TIL YOU'VE SCORED

(cable TV sports program)

LEARN TO HOLD IT UNTIL YOU GET TO THE CAN

(anti-littering campaign)

Seizing on the controversy that erupted when Daryl Gates refused to step down as L.A. police chief, a Chinese restaurant promoted its delivery service with a photo of Gates and a tongue-in-cheek message. Later, the restaurant's billboards commented on the impact of Mexican food on the ozone.

THINK OF THEM AS HUSH PUPPIES IN HEAT

(cowboy boots).

LESS MUSIC BY DEAD GUYS

(radio station).

THE BEST BREASTS IN L.A. WITHOUT PLASTIC SURGERY

(Popeye's Chicken, taken down after protests by breast cancer survivors).

IT PAYS TO BE A B.U.M.

(sportswear ad opposite Skid Row mission for homeless, removed after complaints).

WEATHERPERSON
KNX RADIO
700 CIVIC CENTER DRIVE WEST
SANTA ANA, CA 92701

DEAR WEATHERPERSON,

MY HUSBAND, TO WHOM I WAS MARRIED FOR NEARLY THREE DECADES AND WHO
CHEATED ON ME FOR YEARS, BECAME MY EX-HUSBAND SEVERAL MONTHS AGO.

NOW HE IS GOING TO BE REMARRIED IN A LAVISH OUTDOOR CEREMONY ON
OCTOBER 23RD.

YOU KNOW WHAT TO DO.   MORALLY JUSTIFIED

This revenge-minded request was faxed to the weather forecaster at KNX radio.

Ad in L.A. Press Club magazine makes clear how sheriff's department feels about the media these days.

media

Hello, this is the AP tree...Memorable (and not so memorable) TV **news slogans**...A disc jockey's **exploding toilet hoax**...An obituary for Victor Frisbie, who never really existed...**The blooper file.**

In his book for religion writers, John Dart of the Los Angeles Times mentioned the wacky characters who show up at newspapers. He recalled how a copy messenger disarmed one such visitor. When the religious fanatic said, "You may not believe this, but I am the Messiah," the copy messenger replied: "You may not believe this, but you're the third one today."

▼

After the typewriter company, Smith Corona Corp., filed for bankruptcy, KCAL-TV's Cary Berglund interviewed Angelenos for their reaction. One man told Berglund he had no opinion. Then he added, by way of explanation: "I don't drink."

▼

John Lippman, a news director at KCBS-TV with a sense of showmanship, banned the use of umbrellas on camera by his reporters. Lippman even ordered one high-salaried newsman to make sure that he had stood in the rain for a while before going on the air.

▼

During the 1980 presidential race, the Associated Press needed a place to mount a telephone outside the Pacific Palisades residence of candidate Ronald Reagan. So it paid 50 cents a day to lease an oak tree across the street. When the phone rang, one reporter answered by saying: "AP tree."

In a pre-April Fool's Day hoax, disc jockey Rick Dees told his listeners that a backed-up sewer system in the city could cause their toilets to explode at any minute. He suggested placing 10 pounds of weight on toilet seats as a safety precaution. Whereupon several hundred panicked people phoned L.A. and Orange County public works offices. "I checked and found we had no problems," said one official. "Fortunately, I think a lot of people just decided to go to work rather than stand on their toilet seat all day."

▼

Winnie Ruth Judd

When Winnie Ruth Judd, the so-called "Trunk Murderess," was arrested in 1931 at an L.A. train station, police found a blood-soaked trunk containing human remains. It was a sensational story and newspaper reporters raced to meet their deadlines.

Reporter Warden Woolard called police investigator Bill White, and asked: "Bill, how many bodies are in that trunk?"

"Warden, we don't know," said White. "It's a hell of a mess. Can you call us back in a while?"

Twice more Woolard phoned, only to be put off. Since this was the era of multiple daily editions for newspapers, Woolard was growing more and more frustrated. When a third call to White failed to elicit the number of bodies, the reporter blew up.

"Good God, Bill," Woolard shouted. "Just count the heads!"

▼

Detectives inspect trunks that contained bodies.

A reporter researching a story about murdered prostitutes in South-Central Los Angeles approached a lady of the night there. The media-wise hooker yelled: "Five dollars a question, five dollars a question."

▼

As the Spanish-American War raged in May, 1888, the L.A. Times said it would broadcast bulletins to the city by sounding coded blasts on a loud whistle. The paper suggested that townspeople keep a copy of the code "in your hat" so that they could quickly translate the messages.

without local tv news shows, you'd miss slogans like this

"There's more to life than news, weather and sports." (KABC)

▼

"Who's Maury Povich?" (KNX, now KCBS, advertising an out-of-town hire who was about to take over as anchorman.)

▼

"If you report the news, you have to go where the news is." (KNBC)

▼

"Sometimes, being the only one with all the serious news makes us feel lousy." (KABC)

▼

"The next generation of local news." (KCBS, unveiling a format that lasted six weeks.)

▼

"Killer storms? Yes. Killer Tomatoes? No." (KCBS)

▼

"It's not like watching news, it's like watching family". (KABC)

▼

"Fritz said it would be like this." (KNBC promotion for weatherman Fritz Coleman. The 1985 campaign upset Republicans who said it implied the nation would have fewer economic problems if voters had elected Democrat Walter "Fritz" Mondale to the presidency the year before.)

We knew them when: TV and radio personalities who have switched names:

• Deejay **Art Ferguson** adopted a new name during a stint in Oklahoma City and it's now inscribed on the Hollywood Walk of Fame: Charlie Tuna.

• KNBC-TV's **Kelly Lange** was known as Dawn O'Day when she was a morning traffic reporter at KABC radio in the late 1960s.

• KTLA-TV sportscaster **Stu Nahan** started out as Captain Philadelphia, the host of a cartoon show in that town. In Sacramento, he was Skipper Stu, showing cartoons while piloting a boat.

• This talk show host started at KFI as E.J. Hilliard. It took him a while, he said, to persuade his bosses that it was OK to use his real name: **Joe Crummey**.

TODAY

Mostly cloudy and sunny skies with rain and snow and cold temperatures in the high 90's

WEDNESDAY

Mostly cloudy and sunny skies with rain and snow and cold temperatures in the high 90's

THURSDAY

Mostly cloudy and sunny skies with rain and snow and cold temperatures in the high 90's

FRIDAY

Mostly cloudy and sunny skies with rain and snow and cold temperatures in the high 90's

Who says Southern California doesn't have seasons?

can we try that again?

When he was a KCBS anchorman, a momentarily confused Jim Lampley opened one newscast with the words: "Good evening, I'm Bree Walker." Which came as a surprise to his co-anchor and wife — Bree Walker.

▼

Reported in The Star News, a magazine of the L.A. County Sheriff's Relief Assn.: As a TV reporter concluded his interview with Sgt. Ron Spear at the scene of a homicide in Monterey Park, Spear was surprised to hear the tongue-tied newsman say: "There you have it, folks. The Sheriff's Department is trying to tie Ron Spear to this murder."

▼

A radio news reporter covering a shooting told listeners that police had found "an unarmed baby in the car."

▼

A weather forecast: "Partly sunny tonight and Sunday."

terrible transitions r us

Channel 2 reported a dispute between a woman and a finance company over the seizure of her car by repo men while she was driving on the freeway. Then came a commercial that began: "What would it take to get you out of a Honda Accord?"

▼

A Channel 2 commentary on the execution of murderer Robert Alton Harris was followed by a commercial for Tombstone Pizza, which featured a condemned man being asked: "What do you want on your Tombstone?"

candidate for a bad taste award

When a newspaper in Glendale reported the arraignment of LAPD Officer Laurence Powell in the beating of Rodney G. King, it noted that Powell was a graduate of nearby Crescenta Valley High. The headline on the story read: "Ex-CV High golf star is still swinging."

we'll miss victor

When the Los Angeles Examiner died in 1962, so did Victor Frisbie.

Frisbie was not a real person, but his name had appeared often in the Examiner. Reporters bored with routine assignments regularly made up quotes attributed to Frisbie and sneaked them into stories. Top editors were unaware of the game.

Frisbie was a great fan of the Rose Parade, judging by the number of times he appeared in parade stories—although one account noted that he had been arrested for drunkenness on New Year's Eve.

Then the Examiner folded, and a boxed, one-paragraph story appeared in the last issue. It said simply:

"BAKERSFIELD—Victor Frisbie, well-known sportsman and traveler, died here Friday. He was 58."

spelchek

"Wow! You guys really know how to make a Rob Roy," a reader wrote the Ventura County Star after the newspaper printed this recipe for the drink: **"11 ounces of Scotch and 1 ounce of sweet Vermouth."** Make that 1½ ounces of Scotch and ½ ounce of Vermouth, replied the newspaper in a correction.

A columnist for the San Gabriel Valley Tribune inadvertently omitted one letter from a piece about a local fair, the theme of which was: "Come Take a Peek." He left the "k" out of "Peek."

---

12 SAN JOAQUIN VALLEY: Mostly sunny and slightly cooler today and Tuesday, with highs in the mid-80s to the 90s. Really neat tonight with lows in the mid-50s to the 60s.

Sure sounds neat to us.

song lyrics that immortalize l.a.

It's a long day living in Reseda; there's a freeway running through the yard...
— **Tom Petty**

Rolling down the Imperial Highway with a big nasty redhead at my side...— **Randy Newman**

L.A. is a great big freeway...— **Dionne Warwick**

If I can just get off of that L.A. freeway without getting killed or lost...
— **Jerry Jeff Walker**

Santa Monica Freeway sometimes makes a country girl blue-ooh-ooh...
— **Shelly West**

Thought I'd be a star right away, but I'm sweeping out a warehouse in West L.A...— **Delbert McClinton**

Pico and Sepulveda, Pico and Sepulveda...— **Oingo Boingo**

And loved the world away in Marina del Rey...— **George Strait**

All I wanna do is have some fun until the sun comes up over Santa Monica Boulevard...— **Sheryl Crow**

L.A. proved too much for the man...— **Gladys Knight and the Pips**

Coming into Los Angeles, bringing in a couple of keys.
Don't touch my bags if you please, Mr. Customs Man...— **Arlo Guthrie**

I left my liver in the L.A. River...— **Author unknown**

Some official — and unofficial — songs of Southland communities:

Let's Sing to Glorious Glendora (Where trees in bloom waft their perfume).by Henry Scott Rubel
When Veronica Plays Her Harmonica Down on the Pier at Santa Monica by Kay Kyser
Culver City, I Love You by Marilyn Clark
The Little Old Lady From Pasadena (Go granny, go granny, go granny go!) by Roger Christian and Don Altfeld
Reseda (You won't find a city with rent-a-cheapa) by Susan Dubow
Redondo Beach for a Day or a Lifetime by Peter Hume
City of Industry by Arlon Ober
My Simi Valley by Deana Hardin Merrifield
Christmas in Malibu (St. Nick and his elves, wet suits off the shelves) by Joe Klein

"So I think
I'll just travel on
to Avalon..." —Al Jolson

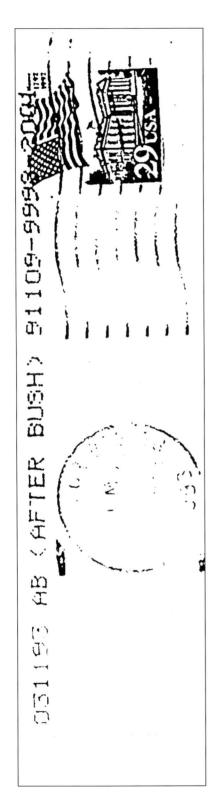

A postal worker's tribute to the President who was ousted by Bill Clinton.

Think **"Dear Occupant"** is an insult? Wait until you read these greetings…When mail is trapped in **the Twilight Zone** (or, the postcard that was 50 years late)…Solving the mystery of E Cikiradi Vkud and other **baffling addresses**.

What you've always suspected about postal rates: In a downtown magazine shop, a stamp machine had this sign: "Out of Control."

▼

The mail solicitation from USC seemed to be properly addressed. But next to the name of the addressee was this notation: "Deceased." Then came the opening sentence: "It has been more than five years since you last supported USC…" Maybe the next of kin weren't forwarding the mail.

▼

A postal patron overheard this request for the new self-adhesive stamps: "I'd like a book of those pre-licked stamps."

▼

Odd items in L.A. mail: an unwrapped automobile tire with stamps on the treads and a properly addressed but bare grapefruit. Both sailed through smoothly, unlike the package of live snakes that burst open. "That had everyone here upset for a while," said a Post Office spokesman.

▼

When a rate increase boosted the price of a stamp book to $5.80, postal workers in Santa Monica faced a dilemma. Their vending machines would not return dimes in change, meaning that

miscelLAny

The county's only carrier-pigeon mail service was inaugurated in 1894 when a bird named Orlando set off from Santa Catalina Island for Bunker Hill. He arrived 54 minutes later with his message. The service continued for a few years until the Pacific Wireless Co. established itself on Catalina, putting the pigeons out of business.

anyone who inserted $6 in currency to buy one of the books would be stiffed 20 cents. The solution: taping two dimes in change to each book. "It's easier to package them with the stamps than retrofitting the machines," said a spokesman. Clerks on limited duty for medical reasons were assigned to the coin-taping detail.

▼

Southern California has traditionally been home to spiritualists, mediums and other mystics. So John McWhorter of Bakersfield shouldn't have been surprised to receive a newsletter from the Los Angeles alumni club of the University of Chicago that asked this question:

"Have you moved or passed on recently?"

▼

Trust your post office: The post-cards that came into the CARE charity in West Los Angeles said something about the honesty of postal clerks. Every week for several years, the cards arrived—with $20 bills stapled to them in plain view. The donor was anonymous.

The man was flailing his arms and cursing at the clerk in an Atwater post office, complaining how inept the operation was. The people waiting in line behind him, aware of episodes of violence in postal settings, stiffened nervously.

But the man confined his anger to words and eventually stalked out.

Afterward, the clerk was asked what the dispute was about.

"Well," she said, "we told him we ran out of Elvis stamps."

hey, age is no problem

When Transamerica Financial Services wrote to Brian Cagle of Westchester, offering to make him a $3,000 loan "in just two working days," family members were frankly surprised. For one thing, he was unemployed and still living at home with his parents. Like most 1-year-olds.

"This is not a misprint," said the computerized offer sent to a Sylmar residence. "Your name, Mr. Marcos Baxter, is definitely on the list which guarantees you will receive certified bank checks from United States Purchasing Exchange for over $2 million." The small print advised Baxter to sign and return an eligibility affidavit. Baxter, unfortunately, couldn't write yet, being only 7 months old.

is there a zip code for the twilight zone?

County animal control officials were mildly irritated when a dog license renewal check written in 1989 arrived in the mail in 1993. Said a spokesman: "To add insult to injury, the 25-cent stamp on the letter was deemed insufficient postage." The cost of a stamp had gone up in the interim.

▼

A picture postcard bearing a one-cent stamp and a Sept. 11, 1939 postmark finally made it to a Manhattan Beach address — 50 years later. The intended recipient, of course, was long gone. Resident Carey Anderson, who discovered the card in her mail, said, "All I can figure is that it just turned up at the post office the other day."

▼

The Christmas card that Dorothy Morris of San Marino received from Atty. Gen. John Van de Kamp was postmarked Dec. 13, 1989, and read: "Have a Good 1990." Fine, except the card arrived in December, 1991.

▼

Pat Stafford of West L.A. decided to try her luck in a radio contest. Following instructions, she addressed a postcard to the station and wrote her address and phone number on the back. The post office mailed the card to her rather than the station. She sent it a second time. Back it came. On her third try, she wrote "Front" on the side with the radio station's address and "Back" on the side with her home address. It was returned again. She gave up.

▼

An envelope that Sara Meric mailed to "City Hall, Santa Monica" came back stamped, "No Such Address."

ALICE C. ▨▨▨▨▨
▨▨▨▨ LAUREL HILLS RD.
STUPID CITY, CA 91604◀▨▨▨

Studio City gets no respect.

could you repeat that address?

Letters with unfathomable street addresses are assigned to the Post Office's "nixie" clerks (derivation of the term is uncertain). These postal sleuths enabled Elizabeth Calciano of Pasadena, for instance, to receive a letter from Hong Kong addressed to her office on "E Cikiradi Vkud." A clerk correctly deduced that the sender had intended to type "E Colorado Blvd." but had inadvertently stationed his or her right hand one key to the left.

Some other triumphs of L.A. nixie clerks:

Roxo (Roscoe)
Queen Bee (Quimby)
Fig Tree (Victory)
Courts (Quartz)
7th Floor 23 (7423)
Big Tree (Victory)
Pawns (Ponce)
Running Nude (Runnymede)

▼

Michael Kirsch of Sherman Oaks recalled his own challenge to the Post Office. While his family was on vacation, "we wanted to send a card to a dear friend in Van Nuys, but we didn't have the address." So Kirsch scrawled the friend's name on the card, followed by this address:

13500 block of Erwin Street
3rd house west of the fire hydrant
South side of the street
Van Nuys, CA 91401

His friend received the card without delay.

---

spelchek

Writer Elliot Zwiebach received a subscription offer from Backstage Magazine declaring that it published **"each and every week, 51 times a year."**

When Vince Pavlicek wrote to a Cleveland company for product information, he was aware that people elsewhere in the U.S. sometimes have trouble spelling Spanish place names. So he was careful to note that his hometown was "L A space J O L L A." You can see the result.

F. VINCE PAVLICEK
UNIV. OF CALIFORNIA SAN DIEGO
MAIL STOP 0704
LOS ANGELES JOLLA, CA   92093

a two-year odyssey

It happened four decades ago, and Peter Winter of La Crescenta had the incredible multi-addressed envelope to prove it. A friend originally mailed the letter to Winter, an Air Force officer during the Korean War.

But Winter was transferred before it arrived. Thus began the letter's odyssey, always one stop behind Winter.

"It showed up after I'd left Mississippi," Winter said. "Then it followed me to Randolph Field in Texas, to North Carolina, to Tennessee and to Japan."

After two years, the letter was returned to the sender, Capt. Leo Dustman, who presented it to Winter at a post-war reunion in New York.

In all, the letter made almost a dozen stops in two years—all on the same 3-cent stamp.

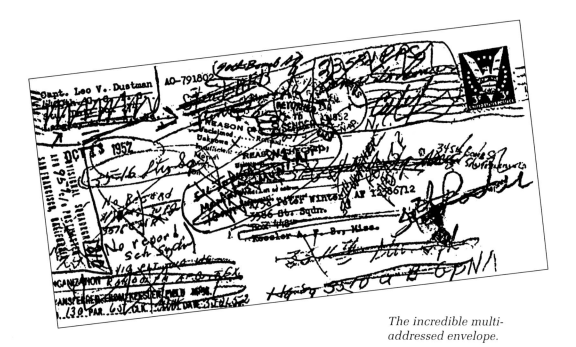

The incredible multi-addressed envelope.

you think 'dear occupant' is bad?

When computers are allowed to write letters and address the mail, there is no telling what will happen:

● Jan Haas of Pacific Palisades got a piece of junk mail addressed to "End of Roll."

● Dean Terlinden received a note from a book club addresssed to: "No Advertising Matter"

● Susan Tellem of Beverly Hills thought it was a bit dehumanizing when the bill from her allergist addressed her as "NO NAME."

● After Nancy Kronick set up a revocable trust, she began receiving letters addressed to: "Revocable Kronick."

```
N. O. Name
█████ Sawtelle Blvd.
Los Angeles, CA  90064-3195

Dear N. Name,

    Your name has been given to us because you have shown a
willingness to help your neighbors in the Los Angeles area.  We
are conducting our 1995 Annual Fund Drive in Los Angeles, and we
are counting on your help today.
```

A computer's personal touch.

Thousands of numbers have already been eliminated from Sweepstakes contention. If one of the numbers on this Audit Control List is the winning number and matches the number on your Data Card

PSYCOEDUCATIONAL ASS HAS BEATEI THE ODDS TO BECOME OUR NEWEST TEN MILLION DOLLAR WINNER!

It's supposed to be Psycoeducational Associates.

```
************5-DIGIT 90004
Ns Senio R. L A Me
531 N. June Street
Los Angeles, CA  90004




Dear Ns Senio R. L A Me:

Since 1852, our commitment at Wells Fargo has been to          come through for our customers.
It is vital that we know how our customers feel about the service we provide to them.
```

Ken Jaffe was baffled by the salutation on this letter — until he realized the computer was trying to make contact with his sports team, the L.A.-Westside Men's Senior Baseball League.

```
Dear Mr. Claude Johnson:

Just return the Grand Prize winning sweepstakes number before August
12, 1994 and you'll be turning quite a few heads on the streets of
Los Angeles as you roar down P.O. Box 3543 in your brand new Callaway
SuperNatural Corvette.
```

Actually, Mr. Johnson says he doesn't see much traffic driving down P.O. Box 3543.

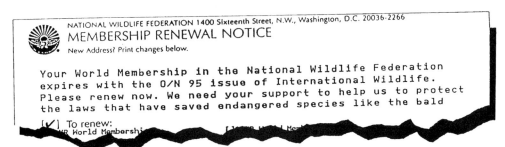

```
NATIONAL WILDLIFE FEDERATION 1400 Sixteenth Street, N.W., Washington, D.C. 20036-2266
MEMBERSHIP RENEWAL NOTICE
New Address? Print changes below.

Your World Membership in the National Wildlife Federation
expires with the O/N 95 issue of International Wildlife.
Please renew now. We need your support to help us to protect
the laws that have saved endangered species like the bald

[✓] To renew:
    ...R World Membershi...                  ...World Mem...
```

Nice to see an organization that cares about hair loss.

```
ꞏePrudential                    The Prudential
                                Insurance Company
                                of America

BURTON L COHEN

SEPULVEDA CA 91343

你有興趣…我們亦有興趣
請逕明您所關切的事項,並用所附免費信封寄回。

                              保天畀財務保險公司(The Prudential)
                              臺灣代表  敬上

姓名    _____
住址    _____
城市    _____  州 ____ 郵政號碼 ____
電話(宅) _____ (公) _____
什麼時候打電話最好 _____
生日:年 _____ 月 _____ 日 _____
配偶的生日:年 _____ 月 _____ 日 _____
請你寄給我下面有( )存覽的資料:
•財産保險            •人壽保險            •地産服務
( )汽車/船艇保險 •    ( )普通保險         ( )買屋服務
( )房屋保險 •        ( )個客保險          ( )賣屋服務
( )百萬家庭責任保險   ( )房屋貸款保險       ( )住宅抵押 †
                                        ( )賣款 †
```

The letter to Burton Cohen was correctly addressed.
It was what followed the salutation that was really strange.

145

schools

Well, there's someone who didn't score 1600 on the SAT.

A scholarship reserved for the student "willing to bite the hand that feeds him"...The shortest ever **graduation speech**...A favorite teacher becomes a **TV sitcom character**...The great flash card caper and other **Caltech stunts**.

Your mistake here: Students learning English at an adult school in Paramount were asked to write letters to the City Council in support of a special parking zone in front of the campus. A sample letter was displayed on the classroom bulletin board. But the instructor apparently didn't explain it fully enough. More than 100 of the letters were signed:

Sincerely yours,
Your Name Here

▼

This note was found on a classroom desk at Belmont High School, apparently written by a student who was asking a classmate to help him with a love letter:

Can you write in Thai, I need you please
and I can't live without you, please?

Below the note was the requested translation in pencil, followed by a somewhat shaky version in ink. Apparently, the infatuated student had practiced writing the words before dispatching the real thing.

▼

Banning High's Val Rodriguez counts this as the most unusual excuse for an absence that he received in 32 years of teaching. On a form asking the reason for not being at school, the student had responded: "Sex."

How do you show your appreciation for a favorite teacher? If you are Christopher Lloyd, an executive produce of TV's "Frasier," you name a sitcom character in his honor. Lloyd named the show's restaurant critic, Gil Chesterton, after his journalism teacher at Beverly Hills High School.

▼

Straying Spouses 101: Billie Long, who worked as a secretary at Pierce College, recalled the time an assistant dean became concerned over the high number of students who signed up for night classes but dropped out after the semester began. The dean sent postcards to each of them, asking why they had quit.

"He soon started to receive telephone calls from very puzzled husbands and wives," said Long. "They didn't understand where he got the idea that their spouse had dropped their classes. Several remarked that their spouse had perfect attendance. The dean promptly decided that it was not a very good idea and wondered how many marriages he had inadvertently broken up."

▼

When humorist Art Buchwald established a scholarship at USC, he set this criteria for the winner: "The student would be anti-establishment, contemptuous of the scholarship and willing to bite the hand that feeds him." One graduate student, taking Buchwald's advice, used his $2,000 award to follow the Grateful Dead from concert to concert.

▼

Three little words: Commencement speaker Richard Moore figured it had all been said by the time his turn came at graduation ceremonies for a private school. Nearly a dozen speakers had preceded him.

So Moore, president of Santa Monica College, walked to the dais, looked out at the spectators and intoned:

"Feelings. Adventures. Ideas."

End of speech.

He received a standing ovation.

This bus stops at all scohols.

The announcement original-ly said, "Save Your Pennies." It was too inviting for one prankster to pass up.

Give me an A—please, will someone give me an A.

Next time, ask the English department to help.

welcome to l.a., kids

For 35 school kids from Calabasas, the highlight of the field trip to downtown L.A. was supposed to be a ride on L.A.'s Red Line subway. But when the bus pulled up in front of Union Station so the kids could catch the subway train, a guard intervened.

"You can't stop here," he said. "Buses have to follow the arrows."

Of course--the arrows.

Unfortunately, the bus driver followed the wrong arrows and ended up on the El Monte Busway, heading east, away from downtown. The kids' unscheduled field trip took them all the way to Alhambra before the bus could turn around. The final insult: by the time they got back downtown, there was no time for a subway ride.

a nasty habit indeed

Don't think for a moment that schools didn't have problems in the old days. One particularly odious activity was singled out in a 1912 newspaper story that condemned it as "unsanitary and unhealthful." The big school problem? Gum chewing.

spelchek

DEAN

SCHOOL OF PUBIC POLICY AND SOCIAL RESEARCH

UNIVERSITY OF CALIFORNIA, LOS ANGELES

UCLA invites nominations and applications for the position of Dean of the School of Public Policy and Social Research. The unique challenge of this position is to provide administrative and academic leadership to develop the teaching, research and public service dimensions of the School, one of the premier schools of it

Ad in the Economist reveals UCLA to be a real innovator.

soup sipping 101

An early 20th Century code of conduct at the all-girl Marlborough School, reprinted in the magazine, The Californians, contained this advice:

"Don't talk about yourself or your family affairs. It is a sign of verdancy.

"Don't be inquisitive with either tongue or fingers. Curiosity is wholly vulgar and common.

"Don't take soup noisily.

"And don't, even once, allow yourself to put celery, Saratoga potatoes, toast, biscuit, or any other crisp eatable into your mouth without closing your lips upon it before you bite it and your teeth upon it before you chew it."

call it caltrick university

Some of the hijinks that have been pulled off by the always creative students of Caltech:

• In 1940, learning that a fellow student needed a car for a Saturday night date, classmates bought a Model T Ford for $9, took it apart, then reassembled it in his room while he was out.

• Caltech pranksters secretly altered the card stunts at the 1961 Rose Bowl causing University of Washington students on game day to unwittingly do this before millions of TV viewers: flash a giant picture of a Husky with rounded ears and buck teeth (suspiciously resembling a Caltech Beaver), spell out WASHINGTON backwards and, of course, spell out CALTECH perfectly.

• Taking advantage of a McDonald's drawing that permitted unlimited entries, a band of students entered 1.1 million times. They won 20% of the prizes, including a new car, prompting McDonald to complain that the Caltekkies didn't play fair.

miscelLAny

Aviator Charles Lindbergh attended Redondo High School for one semester in 1917 during a brief stopover in the area by his family. Young Lindy received high grades in every subject except geometry.

Actors: Robert Blake, Joel Grey, Michele Lee and Rita Hayworth (Hamilton), Lana Turner, Mickey Rooney, Jason Robards and James Garner (Hollywood), Ricardo Montalban (Fairfax), ex-porn star Traci Lords (Redondo), Robert Redford and Stacy Keach (Van Nuys), Alan Arkin (Franklin), Alan Ladd (North Hollywood), Jack Webb (Belmont), Robert Stack (Los Angeles), Sally Field (Birmingham), Richard Dreyfuss and Albert Brooks (Beverly Hills), Sue Lyon and Julie Newmar (Marshall), Laraine Day and Van Heflin (Long Beach Poly), Robert Young (Lincoln).

Musicians/Singers: Frank Zappa (Antelope Valley), Weird Al Yankovic (Lynwood), Jackson Browne (Sunny Hills-Fullerton), Tom and Dick Smothers (Redondo), Marilyn Horne, Jo Stafford and Snoop Doggy Dogg (Long Beach Poly), Herb Alpert (Fairfax), Stevie Nicks (Arcadia), Paula Abdul (Van Nuys), Bobby Sherman (Birmingham), Los Lobos band members Cesar Rosas, Conrad Lozano, David Hidalgo and Louie Perez (Garfield), Natalie Cole (Immaculate Heart), Cher (Montclair), Belinda Carlisle (Newbury Park), Karen and Richard Carpenter (Downey), Rick Nelson (Hollywood).

Screenwriters: Nora Ephron (Beverly Hills).

Dancers: Gwen Verdon (Hamilton).

TV Moguls: Barry Diller (Beverly Hills).

Directors: Penny Marshall (Beverly Hills).

Athletes: Don Drysdale (Van Nuys), Billie Jean King, Tony Gwynn and Gene Washington (Long Beach Poly), Bret Saberhagen (Birmingham), Darryl Strawberry (Crenshaw), Walter Johnson (Fullerton), George "Sparky" Anderson (Dorsey), Sidney Wicks, Warren Moon and Harry "Peanuts" Lowrey (Hamilton).

Broadcasters: Al Michaels (Hamilton), Jim Healy (Beverly Hills).

Diplomats: Warren Christopher (Hollywood).

Conductors: Andre Previn (Beverly Hills).

Nobel Prize winners: Ralph Bunche (Jefferson), Glenn Seaborg (Jordan), William Shockley (Hollywood).

Astronauts: Walter Cunningham (Venice), Sally Ride (Westlake School for Girls), Kevin Chilton (St. Bernard-Playa del Rey), Kathleen Sullivan (Taft).

Judges: Lance Ito (Marshall), Joseph Wapner (Hollywood).

Attorneys: Johnnie Cochran (Los Angeles), Robert Shapiro (Hamilton).

Defendants: Heidi Fleiss and Red Light Bandit Caryl Chessman (Marshall), Michael Milken (Birmingham), Manson girl Squeaky Fromme (Redondo), Erik Menendez (Beverly Hills), Bruce McNall (Arcadia).

Politicians: Sonny Bono (Inglewood).*

* Didn't graduate.

ITO (Marshall)

FLEISS (Marshall)

MILKEN (Birmingham)

DILLER (Beverly Hills)

COLE (Immaculate Heart)

ZAPPA (Antelope Valley)

BONO (Inglewood)

CHER (Montclair)

educating marilyn

Marilyn Monroe attended these L.A. schools, according to film historian Ken Schessler: Washington Elementary (Hawthorne), Vine Street Elementary and Selma Street School (both Hollywood), Sawtelle Elementary and Emerson Junior High (West L.A.), Van Nuys High and University High (West L.A.). She dropped out of University High at the age of 16 to get married.

The real reasons the **Rams** left L.A…How the **Frisbee** got its name and where the **Zamboni** originated…L.A.'s sporting history (before the Dodgers, there were the Tourists)…The origin of "cowabunga" and other **surfing lore**.

Peanuts on ice: The Zamboni, the resurfacing machine used in ice rinks and hockey arenas around the world, was developed a half-century ago in the L.A. suburb of Paramount by inventor Frank Zamboni. The contraption attained folk hero status when it was used as a running gag in the "Peanuts" comic strip. In a typical exchange, Charlie Brown asks Snoopy: "Well, how was hockey practice?" Responds the melancholy hound: "I don't think the coach likes me…He told me to stand in front of the Zamboni."

▼

Three black-clad daredevils waited until after midnight to parachute from a downtown high-rise still under construction. Two made it all the way down; the third hit some trees and ended up on a fourth-floor patio. Some days later, four sky-divers masqueraded as workers to get access to the roof of a 32-story office building, from which they made their jump. All survived without injury.

▼

Wealthy boosters—donating $250,000 each—have "endowed for life" 29 positions on USC's football team, including punter, place-kicker and one special teams player. The gifts cover scholarship and room and board costs for players occupying the positions.

Misinterpreting a city ordinance that prohibited the throwing of objects at sporting events, Dodgers management benched peanut-tosser-extraordinaire Roger Owens. Reinstated later, the popular vendor said of his two-week ban: "It was sad to see the fans holding their hands out."

▼

Golfer Fred Van Allen, playing the Mile Square Course in Fountain Valley, hit a tee shot just short of a sand bunker. A fox emerged from the nearby trees, picked up the ball in his mouth, walked about 15 feet, and then dropped it. "I thought, 'Great, he gives me a better lie,'" said Van Allen. But the fox had one last task to perform: "He takes about half a step, squats over the ball and urinates on it. Then he looks over his shoulder at me and runs off into the lot next door." Van Allen disposed of the ball by smacking it in the direction of the now-vanished fox.

▼

It happened after a Philippine Little League team was disqualified for cheating and a Long Beach team was proclaimed world champion: Long Beach awarded a key to the city to the Philippine sportswriter who uncovered the scandal.

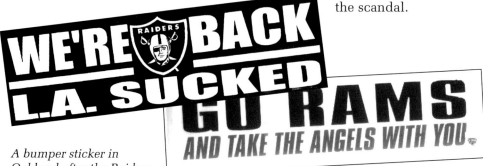

A bumper sticker in Oakland after the Raiders returned from L.A. and a wish that the Rams start a trend with their move out of L.A.

▼

When a verbal spat between Little League managers turned into a fistfight at Sherman Oaks Park, parents spilled out of the stands to join the fracas. Then a quick-thinking groundskeeper turned on the sprinklers. End of brawl.

he wanted to be outta there

Bob Kelley, one of L.A.'s pioneer radio sports-casters, is remembered for his ingenuity. Kelley re-created road games of the minor league Angels in a studio at KMPC. He obtained the play-by-play from Western Union and called the game as if he were there, using various sound effects.

One Sunday, recalled fellow sportscaster Jim Healy, Kelley returned from a local bar to call the second game of a doubleheader.

"And he felt the call of nature—really bad," Healy said.

"But he couldn't leave because there was no one to take his place. Finally, he picked up a metal waste basket and in a few moments he said, 'Uh-oh, folks. It's starting to rain. I think you can hear it coming down on this old tin roof.'"

grandstanding

A survey of spectator eating habits at Dodger games found that general admission fans preferred hot dogs while those in field-level seats favored pizza.

▼

Among those inducted into the USC Athletic Hall of Fame in 1995 was Giles (Super Fan) Pellerin, who had attended 751 consecutive Trojan football games, home and away, since 1926.

▼

An ESPN program about baseball broadcasts credited L.A. fans with originating a now-familiar custom. It was traced to (1) the emergence of an electronics product in the 1950s, (2) the speaking skills of Vin Scully and (3) the large number of undesirable seats in the Coliseum, where the Dodgers first played. The custom: bringing transis-tor radios to the ballpark.

l.a.'s sporting history

The practice of displaying Olympic winners on a victory stand originated at the 1932 Games in L.A.

▼

In keeping with L.A.'s rootless image, the city's professional baseball team at the turn of the century was known as the Tourists.

▼

The first woman licensed to referee a prize fight in the United States was Belle Martell of Van Nuys, who made her debut by working eight bouts in San Bernardino on May 2, 1940.

▼

In 1929, a 188-pound marlin was caught off Catalina Island by a visiting Englishman. Not without some blood, toil, tears and sweat, we'll bet. He was Winston Churchill.

▼

The first quarter of the century was, in many ways, the Golden Era of auto racing in Southern California. Tracks in Corona, Culver City and at the site of the L.A. Coliseum attracted big names like Barney Oldfield and Ralph DePalma. The Vanderbilt Cup races were run on the streets of Santa Monica for four years. And a wood track drew race fans to the then-isolated corner of Santa Monica and Wilshire Boulevards, where the Beverly Wilshire Hotel now stands.

▼

L.A.'s first great horse race occurred on July 4, 1855, when Jose Andres Sepulveda's Black Swan — imported from Australia — raced for 18 miles along San Pedro Street against Pio Pico's California-bred Sarco. The purse: $25,000, plus 500 horses, 500 heifers, 500 calves and 500 sheep. The winner: Black Swan.

surf report

Surfing came to Southern California in 1907 when land developer Henry Huntington brought Hawaiian surfer George Freeth to Redondo Beach. Freeth performed for tourists, using a 200-pound, 8-foot-long wooden board.

▼

According to "The New Book of Rock Lists," only one member of the Beach Boys singing group actually surfed: Dennis Wilson.

▼

The surfing term "cowabunga" came from the '50s-era TV program, "The Howdy Doody Show."

▼

A total of six surfboards are believed to have been in use in L.A. County in 1920.

▼

As a student at Hawthorne High, Beach Boy Brian Wilson failed an assignment in music composition after submitting the song, "Surfin.'" But he managed to get a "C" in the course.

▼

Kathy Kohner Zuckerman, the inspiration for the "Gidget" film character, later managed a restaurant in Santa Monica.

▼

Rhino Chasers, a micro-brewery at LAX's Terminal One, derived its name from the '60s expression for surfers who chased the biggest waves.

the list that swung the rams deal?

Fans in St. Louis were amused by a David Letterman-style list that circulated in the city before the Rams moved there. These were said to be the top five reasons for the team's defection from L.A.

• "Rams merchandise and clothing never caught on with L.A. street gangs."

• "L.A. night life isn't the same with Heidi Fleiss out of business."

• "Players growing tired of relying on mudslides to put out wildfires near their homes."

• "Rams games no longer broadcast in L.A. since televised beatings were banned after the Rodney King video."

• "Instead of socializing with fake L.A. crowd, Rams owner Georgia Frontiere can socialize with fake St. Louis crowd."

come fly with us

A TWA flight from New York to Burbank in the early 1930s was a test of endurance. On the first leg, the plane touched down at five cities en route to Kansas City, where the 11 passengers spent the night. The next day, the plane made three stops before finally reaching Burbank—36 hours after leaving New York.

What do United Airport, Union Air Terminal and Lockheed Air Terminal have in common? All were previous names of Burbank-Glendale-Pasadena Airport, also known as Burbank Airport.

• A United Airlines flight waiting to leave Burbank was already two hours behind schedule. Finally, the pilot got permission to pull away from the gate and taxi to the runway. And taxi. And taxi. "I know some of you are in a hurry to get to San Francisco," the pilot finally said. "I just want to assure you that we'll be picking up speed as soon as we make our way to the 101. And we'll be stopping for pie and coffee along the way."

• On April Fool's Day, Hollywood Park attempted to trick passengers flying into nearby LAX by hoisting a banner that said "Welcome to Chicago" in 20-foot-high red letters.

• Rep. Bob Dornan (R-Garden Grove) was booted off a United Airlines flight for refusing to bring his seat upright for the takeoff. Dornan claimed he had a sore hip.

• An L.A. lawyer was arrested and handcuffed for petty theft— for bringing his own earphones to listen to a movie soundtrack on a United Airlines flight. The charge was later dropped. The movie: "Presumed Innocent."

• A USAir flight out of L.A. made such a rocky landing that overhead bins flew open, prompting a flight attendant to announce, "Well, now that the pilot has finished engraving his initials on the runway, we can welcome you to San Francisco!"

• A Southwest Airlines flight to L.A. was taking an unusually long time taxiing to the gate after the landing. That inspired a flight attendant to announce: "Now you know why we are called low-fare Southwest Airlines. We fly you halfway and drive you the rest."

The city of El Segundo, angry at the noise from planes departing nearby LAX, erected this large sign that could be viewed by outbound pilots and passengers. City officials agreed to cover the sign after LAX promised to try a different takeoff procedure. The message was mild compared to others that were considered. Among the rejects: TURN AT THE COASTLINE, STUPID.

Royal ♔ Caribbean

Attention Orange County Airport...
You've Got Some Royal Caribbean Coming!

Due to a deluge of requests from you,
our travel partners,
we are pleased to announce:

a "New" Air/Sea Gateway

Orange County, California
Wayne Newton Airport

The real reason airline meals aren't always so great?

The Duke wouldn't like this.

The Freeway Chickens.
See page 164.

animals

L.A.'s **most fashionable dog names**…Minnie and her freeway chickens…How to revive a **water-logged iguana**…Please don't call **Lassie** a "she"…**What every pet needs** (the frequent flyer program sounds like a real bargain).

After Kings hockey fans threw live chickens onto the ice, the city of Inglewood made it illegal to toss objects that cause a "disruption of sports and/or entertainment events" at public arenas.

▼

During a Hollywood rehearsal for an Academy Awards telecast, belly-dancer Veena Bidasha's python disappeared. Bidasha camped overnight in the studio in hopes the snake would appear, but to no avail. Finally, five months later, the python was recaptured near the stage for the "Empty Nest" TV show. "She looks great," a spokeswoman said. "We think she may have been hibernating."

▼

L.A. animal shelters imposed a $15 fee for adopting rabbits or poultry after discovering that people were claiming the creatures at no cost—and then cooking them.

▼

Passengers in the waiting room at Union Station were alarmed to see a man firing what appeared to be a rifle at the ceiling. Within moments, security officers were on the scene. But the rifleman was allowed to leave—with his pellet gun—after he explained that it was his job to shoot pigeons that wandered into the large, high-ceilinged room. "We usually schedule indoor work only when it's empty," an apologetic official explained.

miscelLAny

Blackie, the L.A. Fire Department's last horse, died in 1939.

The Long Beach Airport Marriott Hotel posted a warning that pets were not allowed in the hot tub.

▼

A pot-bellied pig running loose in Pasadena had police stumped for a while. Then they put down a trail of cake crumbs leading to the back seat of a patrol car, and the pig ate his way into custody. "He was sitting on the back seat kind of oinking and snorting," one officer proudly reported.

▼

Animal control workers received a call from a woman who wanted to get a marriage license for a male and a female cat "before they breed."

please, no chicken jokes

It's one of L.A.'s most enduring traffic mysteries. During the 1970s and '80s, a band of chickens could be seen roosting in the bushes along a stretch of the Hollywood Freeway.

One story held that the Freeway Chickens were the survivors of a 1960s poultry truck crash. A Granada Hills man claimed the chickens were dumped there by his wife and her sister who, as children, had rescued them from a school that was closing. A Hollywood resident said no, they were his birds—chased off by his pit bull. And a North Hollywood man said the chickens were pets that he and his brother abandoned after complaints from neighbors.

Whatever their origin, the 50-odd birds were fed for years by Minnie Blumfield, who lived nearby and came to be known as the Chicken Lady. After she died, animal control workers rounded up the flock for resettlement on a farm.

Minnie

But passersby later reported that some birds had eluded their captors. "They're very funny," said one motorist. "They walk along on the shoulder, paying no attention to the cars."

A movie script about the saga never made it to the screen. But there was a video game, "Freeway Chickens," in which motorists received points for running over the title characters.

Where dogs and homeowners are involved, snits happen. Perhaps the most creative sign of all was posted by Milton Kagen of Hollywood, a warning that his plants were sprayed with "dioxinleucomaine." No mutts left deposits on Kagen's lawn after that. "Dioxinleucomaine," he later confessed, was a word he made up.

sit, madonna!

Even in glitzy L.A., dogs are still named Fido, Rover and Spot. But other names have become more fashionable, according to dog license records:

Most common names—Lady, Max, Brandy, Rocky, Bear, Princess, Duke, Ginger, Lucky, Blackie, Pepper, Sandy, Sam, Samantha, Muffin, Sheba, Shadow, Coco, Maggie, Missy, Tiger.

Mutts named for celebrities—Madonna, Houdini, Al Capone, Gretzky, Prince Charles, Princess Di, Bob Barker, Elvis, Zsa Zsa, Greta Garbo, Vanna White, Jerry Brown, George Bush, Bo Jackson, Reggie Jackson, Aaron Spelling, Chairman Mao, George Putnam, Donna Rice, Woody Allen, Sylvester Stallone.

Most Eye-Catching Names—Apricot Moose, Smut the Mutt, Cat, Did He Bite, Cocaine, Trust No Friend, L.A. Puke, Rolex, Hey You.

True L.A. names—Freeway, 405, On Ramp, Tail Light, Ozone, Smog, Hollywood, Quake.

Notice posted in Venice: "Lost: 9-inch red-leg tarantula. Answers to the name 'Ralph.' The children have become very attached to 'Ralph' and are inconsolable."

celebrity animals

June Lockhart, who acted in the "Lassie" TV show for six years, confirmed the gossip that had long circulated through Hollywood. All the dogs that portrayed the brave female star of the show were males. "Male dogs are easier to train," Lockhart explained. "They're bigger and they don't have the problem, to delicately put it, of coming into season."

▼

This cat was first thought to be a female. When its finder later discovered it was a male, the ad was revised accordingly. But somebody forgot to delete the phrase "very pregnant."

Animals buried at Los Angeles Pet Memorial Park include Rudolf Valentino's dog Kabar, Charlie Chaplin's cat Boots, Humphrey Bogart's dog Droopy, Hopalong Cassidy's horse Topper, and Mae West's monkey, whose name seems lost to history.

▼

Stuffed animals on display at the Roy Rogers Museum in Victorville include the cowboy star's horses Trigger and Trigger Jr., his dog Bullet, and Dale Evans' faithful mount Buttermilk.

▼

A colony of ants knocked out several traffic lights in Temple City after eating their way through electric wires. They gained national reknown after broadcaster Paul Harvey told his listeners about their "power lunch."

spelchek

If you're looking for a pet that just loafs around, this is for you.

ouch!

Dog breeds with the highest bite rates in L.A., according to a six-year survey: American Staffordshire Terriers (pit bulls), Staffordshire Bulls, German Shepherds, Doberman Pinschers, Collies, Labrador Retrievers, Cocker Spaniels, Dachshunds, Golden Retrievers and Poodles, in that order.

to the rescue

Boa constrictors turn up in the most unexpected places. In Long Beach, lifeguards pulled one out of the L.A. River. Another had to be rescued after entering the plumbing system of an apartment via a toilet bowl. Workers cut open a wall and severed a pipe, and the relieved boa dropped into a waiting duffel bag.

▼

When he saw Rambo, his pet iguana, lying motionless in the family pool, 8-year-old Alex Shindel of Whittier fished the creature out and started blowing air into its mouth. His father, a surgeon, tried a few chest compressions and pronounced Rambo a goner. But Alex kept blowing and that was all Rambo needed. "Pretty soon his leg moved," a surprised Dr. Shindel recounted. "Then his eyes opened." Rambo's recovery was complete.

A solution to junk mail? Sign on a fence in Hollywood: "Please don't throw the mail over. The dogs eat it."

what every pet needs

An airline with a frequent flier program for pets offered a free round trip for every 10 round trips that were paid.

▼

A Burbank boarding facility for cats claimed to be the first to offer "Cat-TV." It was a 1,500-gallon aquarium filled with fish and placed safely behind the concierge's desk.

▼

An animal disposal service offered to cremate a pet and then deliver the ashes to the owner's home in a metal tin. Cost: $50 to $100, depending on the size of the animal.

> PIT BULL
> ON
> ANGEL DUST

Warning sign at Burbank residence.

the Bunyans, paul and pauline

The giant fiberglass creatures looked like something out of a sci-fi movie. They stood guard over a Carson golf course, an East L.A. gas station, a Long Beach lumber yard, a Van Nuys tire shop and a Malibu restaurant.

They were the handiwork of Steve Dashew, whose Venice company began manufacturing the 20-foot-tall figures in the early 1960s. The first one was built for an Arizona restaurateur who wanted a Paul Bunyan mascot to attract passing motorists. Word spread and soon businesses across the nation were asking Dashew to fashion Bunyan siblings—golfers, spacemen, pirates, cowboys and Indians. There was even a Paulina Bunyan, a Miss Uniroyal, who wore a plastic bikini.

"We were constantly making axes," recalled Dashew. "Wherever we had a lumberjack, college kids would steal his ax."

Over time, stricter sign standards reduced the Bunyan population. Some disappeared. Some learned to be flexible. Frosty Man, for instance, became Sombrero Man when his ice cream shop became a Mexican restaurant.

The Southland Bunyans even earned screen credits. Tire Man, for one, went on location for a TV producer. Recalled his former owner: "They cut him down and took him up into the Angeles Forest for an episode of 'The A-Team.'"

LEFT *When Chicken Boy lost his roost on Broadway near 5th Street in downtown L.A., he was purchased by a design firm. Now, the 23-foot-tall figure makes occasional public appearances and promotes his catalog of Chicken Boy products. Among the items: Chicken Boy headwear complete with beak.*
OPPOSITE *A member of the Bunyan clan.*

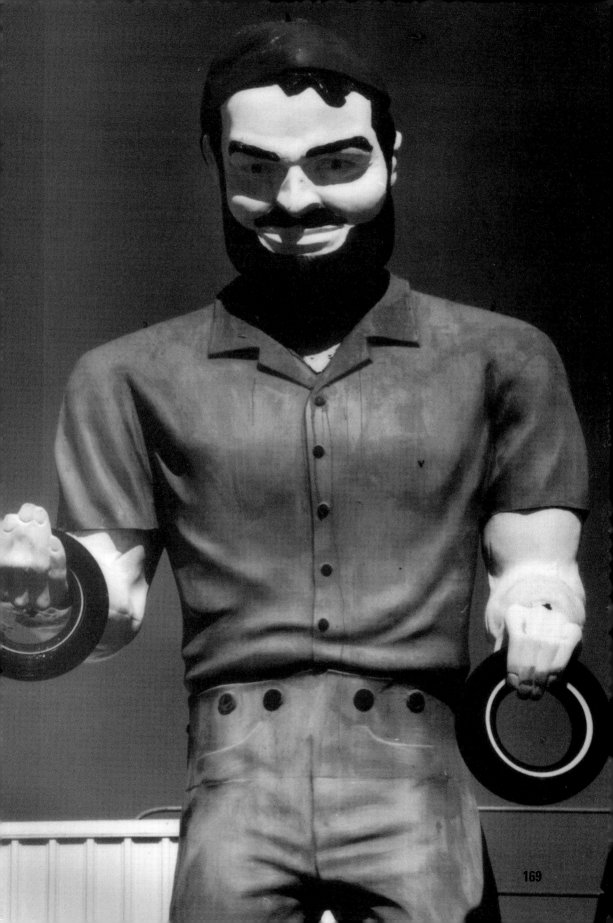

They're better with digits than letters.

The wrong-way McDonald's… **Signs to shop by**…Telephone operators who use aliases…Where Laura Scudder cooked her first batch of chips…Trust those chores to a **nude handyman**…Are these advertisements for real?

Encino's amazing wrong-way McDonald's: Its drive-thru lane was built with the order window on the wrong side of the building because a patio was in the way. Drivers who were alone had to reach through the passenger window for their food.

▼

TRW employees in Redondo Beach planning a Christmas party asked area businesses to contribute money for door prizes "in the spirit of the holiday season." And who would be the needy recipients of the prizes? Some 200 of TRW's finance executives. One party planner said the letter grew out of a tradition at TRW to see who could "have the best parties." A company Scrooge shut down the fund-raising drive.

▼

A fax arrived at a downtown business office with the following notation: "Please advise if not received."

▼

We bet she would have preferred flowers: Sherman Kappe of Cerritos saw this reminder at the bottom of a bill he received: "Don't forget your sweetheart on 2-14-95." The bill was from his exterminator.

miscelLAny

Two names that once meant what they said: (1) Dollar Rent-A-Car, which opened in L.A. in 1956 and offered a Volkswagen bug for $1 a day. (2) The Motel 6 chain, which began in Santa Barbara in 1962 and priced its rooms at $6 per night.

Potato chip mogul Laura Scudder cooked her first batch in Monterey Park in 1926.

Travel writer Norm Sklarewitz of West Hollywood received a press release from SkyWest Airlines heralding company efforts to improve "communication and efficiency." The next day, he received another copy of the press release. And another. And another. In all, he received 26 copies from thorough, if not always efficient, SkyWest.

▼

The checks of an L.A. lawyer listed him as:

Julian Nguyen
Attorney at Law

So, naturally, First Interstate Bank sent him two ATM cards. One was made out to "Julian Nguyen," the other to "Attorney at Law."

▼

It all adds up: The California Society of Certified Public Accountants, in a monthly dues notice to members, listed fees of $50 plus $10, for a total of $70.

Responding to a complaining patron's suggestion, the president of the downtown Kawada Hotel wrote: "Your comment encourages me to begin studying whether or not it is feasible…The study is not complete yet and so far, to tell you the truth, the indication is not very positive but I promise you that your concern is mine." The issue: whether the bar in the hotel restaurant should resume offering mixed nuts.

▼

Sign of the times? The Joy of Learning, an educational bookshop in Tarzana, was replaced by a store selling comic books and toys.

An impossible deadline: "I tried, but I just missed it," said Derek Lovett, referring to a loan application from Manufacturer's Bank that was supposed to be submitted "between the months of November and December."

▼

Aware that the Chinese character for "eight" also means "luck," a bank targeted Chinese-American customers by offering checking account numbers that began with 888, rather than the usual three-digit code for the customer's branch.

The counter sign at Letitia Mills' repair shop in Mar Vista said: "Machines with cockroaches, minimum labor $55. Live or dead bugs." It was no joke. "They live in items that have heat, like answering machines left on 24 hours a day, fax machines, VCRs," explained Mills. "If you open up an answering machine before lunch and find a family of roaches, you don't want to eat."

▼

Upon obtaining a second fax machine in its L.A. office, Tony Stone Worldwide photo library sent out a press release announcing: "We are now bifaxual."

unusual enterprises

The phone number on the side of Vidal Herrera's van read (800) AUTOPSY and advertised a real business: private autopsies and the removal of organs for medical research, among other services. Herrera shunned advertising at first. "But then I saw all the 800 ads on TV and thought, why not?" he said. "Business has gone up at least 50% since then." Not all the attention is positive. One restaurant made him move his van to a less visible parking space. "They said it was in bad taste."

▼

A "Nude Handyman — for Women Only" flyer in Pasadena advertised yard work and repair services, then added: "Also available for parties."

▼

DEPT. OF REDUNDANCY DEPT.

Sign at Holloway Cleaners in West Hollywood: **"Open 7 Days a Week, Sundays Too"**

A beauty salon inside the Northridge Pistol and Rifle Range? "The owner wanted to be in a unique location," explained Renee Saunders, manager of the Bang! Bang! salon. Besides, "when you've had some real crotchety customers, it's a good way to blow off steam after work," she said.

A logical thing to do when overstocked with whites.

Don't even ask about Monday.

signs to shop by

Seen in a Tarzana toy store window: "DIVORCE SALE—Wife has forced husband out of business."

▼

The Northridge Fashion Center posted a code of conduct warning shoppers, among other things, not to engage in "any unnecessary staring" and not to bring in "animals, living or dead."

▼

A Studio City floral shop displayed a sign reading: "Diamonds Only Last Forever—Send Something That Dies."

▼

If you think their oranges are obnoxious, you should see their bananas.

Considering the purpose of the form, Wolcott's stationery store downtown couldn't be blamed for posting this announcement on its counter: "No bankruptcy kits sent out C.O.D. (cash on delivery)—except to law firms."

▼

A Target store in Long Beach earned the gratitude of shoppers with small children by operating a checkstand with a sign that read: "No Candy Displayed in This Lane."

fone follies

After neighborly Pacific Bell said it would allow information operators to identify themselves by their first names instead of by numbers, a caller encountered an operator with an unusual name. "Oh, it's not my real name," the operator confided. "None of us use our real names." A Pac Bell spokesman confirmed that some operators use an alias for reasons of privacy or to avoid being confused with another operator with the same name.

▼

General Telephone was forced to paste over the Olympic rings depicted on the covers of 250,000 L.A.-area directories in 1984 after the U.S. Olympic Committee threatened to sue for unauthorized use of the symbol.

▼

Two-thirds of all phone numbers in the L.A.-Long Beach area are unlisted, according to a study by Survey Sampling Inc.

▼

It's the fear of every caller who suspects the information operator didn't try hard enough. After John Stein of West Los Angeles gave an operator the name of the person he was trying to reach, he was told there was no listing. Unconvinced, he dialed directory assistance again and repeated his request. The operator checked and said, "Still no listing."

DEPT. OF REDUNDANCY DEPT.

An ad for a travel service touted its L.A. to Honolulu flights as **"non-stop."**

spelchek

The UCLA Daily Bruin advertisement for an espresso bar manager said applicants should be "responsible and punctual," adding: **"Conscious a big plus."**

A classified ad for a structural engineer said he or she **"must be expendable."**

A newsletter announced that the Cafe Pinot Downtown was offering a **"French brassiere-style"** setting.

A Northridge firm's flyer pledged that it employed only **"contentious"** painters.

A tax preparer who knows what the IRS is thinking.

175

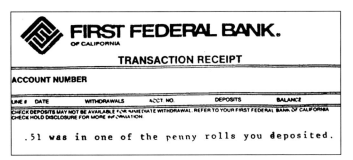

FIRST FEDERAL BANK.
OF CALIFORNIA

TRANSACTION RECEIPT

ACCOUNT NUMBER

LINE #	DATE	WITHDRAWALS	ACCT. NO.	DEPOSITS	BALANCE

CHECK DEPOSITS MAY NOT BE AVAILABLE FOR IMMEDIATE WITHDRAWAL. REFER TO YOUR FIRST FEDERAL BANK OF CALIFORNIA CHECK HOLD DISCLOSURE FOR MORE INFORMATION.

.51 was in one of the penny rolls you deposited.

A bank that keeps track of every penny.

Professional Housecleaning
Houses • Apartments • Condominiums • Offices
7 Days a Week
15 Years Experience • Licensed & Certified

We Clean Entire Resident !

The ultimate extra.

Secretary/Asst

Needed for fast-paced entertainment office. Temp position could lead to f/t permanent. WordPerfect 5.1, typing 60 wpm, excellent organizational skills a **must,** detail oriented, self-starter, ability to work under pressure. Legal firm experience helpful. Starting salary $400/week.

No "Fart-A-Thons" Need Apply!

CLEAN SWEEP CARPET CARE

DOLLAR SAVER

Carpet Steam Cleaning $**15** Per Room

WHEN WE SAY $15 PER ROOM... WE MEAN $115 PER ROOM!

That's what we thought you meant.

Let's not get too formal here.

Typewriter, manual, Royal, types curses

An adults-only machine—or is its
typeface simply "cursive?"

CONCERTS TO GO
BARBEQUE & CLASSICAL
CHAMBER MUSIC FOR
ALL OCCASIONS
Flute. Guitar. Harp.
String Quartet. Harpsichord, Etc.
Serving Greater Los Angeles
. . . . 213 851-7319

Susan Shapiro's ad was supposed to say
"Baroque and Classical."

COMMUNICATIONTIONS WRITER

California's largest trade association
has a new, entry-level position for a
deadline oriented feature and new
writer. Multi-tasked position invloves

That's easy for them to say.

A fruit drink definitely not
served before its time.

WAREHOUSE Ship/Rec. Clerk
wanted must have great organ..

We beg your pardon!

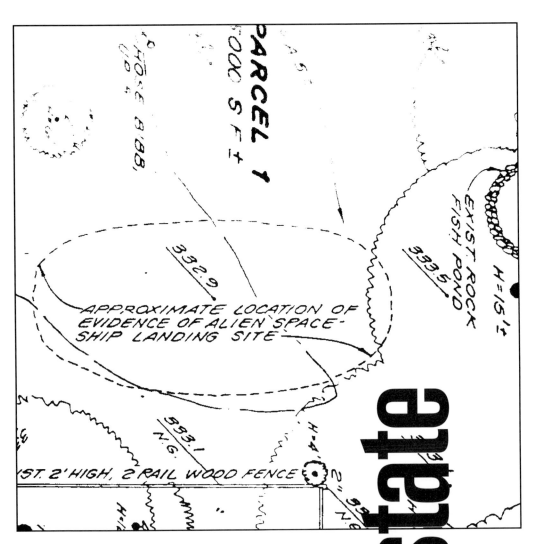

Look closely and you can see the landing site of an alien spaceship on this parcel map for land in Baldwin Park. Actually, it was a joke played by an engineer for developer James Gianni of Glendale. "These parcel maps are jammed so full of information, he wondered if anyone would read all the stuff," Gianni explained.

real estate

Inside the **Skinny House** (it's 10 feet wide)…The talking real estate sign and other **sales gambits**…Where the most bathrooms are…**Listings** you won't want to miss…When a city lot could be had for 63 cents in back taxes.

After a West L.A. couple listed their home for $550,000, a professor newly arrived in L.A. came to look. The wife showed him around while the husband remained in the garage, working on his classic MG. A couple of days later, the professor made his offer: $450,000. And, he said, he wanted the MG.

▼

Karen and Richard Carpenter, the brother-sister singing team reared in Downey, acquired property in the area that they named after one of their hits—the Close to You Apartments.

▼

A Westside couple bought a $1-million property, but didn't like the house. It was too small for their taste, and the interior seemed shabby, especially the furniture left behind by the previous owners. The solution was obvious. The new owners had the whole thing bulldozed: house, furniture, drapes, plants, everything. The next day, they posed for a lighthearted photo among the ruins— on the bulldozer.

▼

Long Beach lays claim to the narrowest free-standing dwelling—the Skinny House, as it's affectionately known. The three-story Tudor-style structure on Gladys Avenue is 10 feet wide, just enough to accommodate double doors in the front. It was built in 1932 by one Newton Rummond, who bet a friend he could squeeze a house into a 10-foot-by-50-foot lot. His creation earned a mention in Ripley's "Believe It or Not."

▼

A one-bedroom, two-bath house in an upscale Santa Monica neighborhood was listed at $1.5 million. If that seemed a bit much, the ad offered this reassuring advice: "Tear down existing structure and build your dream house."

▼

The agent placing this ad seemed a bit unsure about the property: "Is it a house? Is it a lot? A barely inhabitable 1-bedroom home on a desirable lot with alley access in an up-and-coming part of Venice." Price: $295,000.

▼

A rental ad in the Hollywood Reporter boasted that the lucky occupant would be able to "walk to Spago."

▼

A for-rent ad placed by the owner of a North Hollywood house sounded like a great deal: "$50 Week…TV, stereo, shower, phone, nr stores/ bus." Especially if you didn't mind the other condition: "Sleep on couch."

spelchek

ROOM FOR RENT NEAR THIRSTY CLUB - front restroom in large 2 bedroom house private phoneline, cable TV, completelyfurnished - Non-smoker need NOT apply !

At least you wouldn't have a long walk to the toilet.

The kitchen has a butler's panty oak cabinets and granite counters. There is a hardwood floor in the breakfast room.

Just so he keeps it concealed.

sales gambits

Anyone trying to sell real estate during the recent slump in L.A. had to be especially resourceful. Some examples:

• A Cheviot Hills owner staged an essay contest in hopes of selling his $800,000 home. Anyone could compete by paying a $100 entrance fee and submitting a "skill-oriented essay." Problem was, the owner needed 6,750 entrants to make the numbers work. The contest fell through. There just weren't enough essayists out there.

• Several business cards bearing the name of a Santa Monica real estate agent were found in the city's public library, inserted between the pages of such books as "How to Cash in On the Coming Housing Boom."

• A Manhattan Beach man whose home was on the market for $669,000 posted a sign that said: "Dropping Our Price $1,000 a Day or 69 Cents a Minute." Naturally, no one bit right away—or later, for that matter. After 70 days, he quit dropping the price.

• In Encino, the houses themselves spoke through recording devices embedded in the lawn signs. "The house told me the price was $399,000," reported visitor Greg Horbachevsky. "I told it, 'I can't hear you.'"

• One real estate agent laminated his business cards so that he could hand them out to bathers at hotel swimming pools in Beverly Hills and another tried to drum up business by offering a free screening of the movie, "Robin Hood."

• Then there was the candid approach on a flyer for a $449,000 Silver Lake house. At the bottom, it said: "Does anybody read these things? Come on, sell this house and save owner's neck."

A house for sale in Torrance came complete with **"walking closets."**

The features listed in an ad for a mobile home included a **"putty green."**

We knew the market was tough, but: The caption beneath a newspaper photograph of three real estate agents and their trophies said they had been honored **"for sales of $5 in the year."**

1 BATHROOM
LOT SIZE 6,300
SQ. FT. 720

(REALTOR)
24 Hour Vice Mail:

How does he keep his license?

The occupant is over there, behind the tree.

good neighbors

The owners of a house listed for $500,000 found they had an aesthetic problem when it came time for potential buyers to visit: a woman was living in a car near their front yard. In fact, she had been camping out there for several years.

The couple offered the woman $100 to take a vacation. She indignantly refused, telling the couple: "You haven't been good neighbors. You've never even invited me into the house. You're so chummy with the other neighbors. And you've known me longer than them."

A few days later, the car-dweller, apparently recovered from her snit, gave the couple the name and phone number of someone who might want to buy the house. It was the neighborly thing to do.

early lessons in real estate

In 1859, pioneer Henry Hancock offered a company 110 acres of downtown land between Washington and Pico Boulevards to settle a debt. Author Harris Newmark writes that the company chose "to take firewood instead."

▼

In the 1860s, author Oliver Carlson relates, the bottom fell out of the real estate market, leaving many land barons impoverished. At a sheriff's sale of confiscated downtown property, there were no takers for lots on the corners of Main and 5th Streets, Spring and 5th Streets, and Broadway and 4th Street. The asking price for each: 63 cents in back taxes.

▼

An 1892 property tax receipt shows that attitudes about paying the tax collector haven't changed much over the years. The landowner, Vicente Perez, was living on property in San Pedro that had been appraised at $56. He was taxed 67 cents for the land, plus 8 cents for a "special school tax." But Perez shrewdly elected to pay an installment of 38 cents in November and another 37 cents the following June. Why pay the whole thing in November and let the county collect the extra interest on the 37 cents?

But does he do windows? A West L.A. high-rise condo development offered buyers a four-course dinner for six designed by the building's "Cordon Bleu chef Derek Chadwick," complete with crystal, fine china, linens and fresh flowers. Anyone with a complaint about the service could take it to the building's security chief. That was also chef Chadwick.

An L.A. condo owner who had refurbished his units posted a sign that said: **"Regrand opening."**

the definition of a tight market

From Arthur C. Verge's history of L.A. during World War II: Housing shortages were so serious that one newspaper reporter, arriving at the scene of a murder, ignored the corpse and asked the victim's landlady if he could rent the now-vacant apartment. Replied the landlady: "Sorry, I already rented it to that police sergeant over there."

menus, please

Grilled Chicken Breath. Served with Roasted Bell Pepper, Garlic, Onion, French Fries
and Balsamic Glaze...9.95
Grilled eggplant and Red Onion with Basil, Musroom, Bell Pepper

At least this delicacy is low in calories.

DEAREST GRAB LEGS ....
Deep fried crab leg meat and vegetable tempura style served with sweet chili sauce.

X-rated dish?

Sweat and Sour Fish 7.95

A fish with a heavy workout regimen.

41. - Stir Fried Chicken (Human Style)*................................. 6.50

Just so it isn't overcooked.

LIVE MARYLAND
SOFT SHELL CRABS

Piccata Style with Past   Only **$13.90**

A meal that requires a background check.

Sauteed surgeon served on a tomato and zucchini ratatouille

Perhaps a patient's revenge.

```
Chicken (Thing or Leg) .................80
```

Could we ask what kind of thing?

```
PASTA DuJOUR:        SPAGHETTINI WITH BALLS        $12.00
```

A real macho pasta plate.

Fillet of Fist w/ Tomato Basil - $3.50 to - $2.25 • Tostada - $2.25 1.95 • BBQ Beef on a roll -$2.75

This dish packs a punch.

Daily lunch Special 12PM-4PM

Friday- Egg fool young.

It may not be the smart thing to order.

*73. SPICY CALM   9.95
    With sliced chilli, green onion, mint leaves and spicy sauce.

74. CALM IN OYSTER SAUCE   9.95
    With oyster sauce and green onion

Doesn't sound all that spicy.

Evidence that the road to Hell is paved by fast food joints?

restaurants

The hot dog stand that became Carl's Jr. and other **pioneer eateries**... **Famous first dishes**, from the hot fudge sundae to the Cobb salad...The restaurant that never had a name...**Waiters with attitude**...The great French dip debate.

Can You Be More Specific? A sign at the front of Clifton's cafeteria downtown read: "It takes about 11 minutes from this point to be served and reach the cashier."

▼

At the Genghis Cohen restaurant in the Fairfax area, a footnote was added to the usual warning about alcoholic beverages causing birth defects during pregnancy. It read: "Please refrain from any acts that may cause pregnancy while on the premises."

▼

After Zsa Zsa Gabor was convicted of slapping a Beverly Hills police officer who pulled over her Rolls-Royce, a Melrose Avenue restaurant saluted her and a fellow defendant, New York hotel queen Leona Helmsley. The restaurant created a dish featuring two varieties of shellfish bound together by tiny handcuffs: Lobster Zsa and Lobster Leona.

▼

A North Spring Street cafe went 41 years without a name. "People would call it the Corner Cafe, the Ham House, all sorts of things," recalled waitress Lois Fuentes. "But Nick (the owner) was afraid if he gave it a name it might bring in more people. 'Then you gotta hire more help,' he'd say." After Nick Viropolous retired, the eatery was purchased by two Los Angeles police officers who christened the place "Nick's" in his honor.

from small beginnings

These restaurant chains got their start in L.A., sometimes with different names and menus:

Maybe it's time for a name change.

McDonald's. Brothers Richard and Maurice McDonald opened their first eatery near a race track in Arcadia in 1937, followed by a second one in San Bernardino in 1940. McDonald's biographer John Love points out that the original stand served hot dogs, but no hamburgers. The first Golden Arches architecture appeared in 1953.

Carl's Jr. (originally The Blimp). Founder Carl Karcher began with a hot dog stand at Florence and Central Avenues bought in 1941 for $326 and named in honor of a nearby landing strip.

Marie Callender's. She opened her first pie shop in Long Beach, 1948.

Bob's Big Boy (Bob's Pantry). Launched in Glendale, 1936, by Bob Wian, who is credited with the invention of the double-deck hamburger.

Also: **Winchell's**, Temple City, 1948; **Denny's** (Danny's Donuts), Lakewood, 1953; **The Wienerschnitzel**, Wilmington, 1961; and **In-N-Out Burger**, Baldwin Park, 1948.

Ham, Turkey *(Sandwich)*

Millie's Grinder *(Sandwich)*

Shit on a Shingle *(Turkey)*

At Millie's, a down-to-earth restaurant in Silver Lake, the menu once included this chipped-meat-on-toast dish with a raunchy name that ex-GIs would recognize.

famous first dishes

The C. C. Brown ice cream shop in Hollywood claims it invented the hot fudge sundae in 1906 at its original location at 7th and Hill streets.

▼

Victoria Arroyo, who operated a five-seat hot dog stand on East lst Street in the 1930s, introduced the burrito to L.A., according to Westways magazine. It happened when she was out of hot dogs but remembered "a concoction made by her mother from chilies or beans and cheese wrapped in a tortilla."

▼

Robert Cobb, owner of the Brown Derby in Beverly Hills, is credited with inventing the "Shirley Temple" drink for children and the salad that bears his name.

▼

From author Gloria Ricci Lothrop: "In 1935, Art Elkind sold both hot dogs and chili from his pushcart in Inglewood. When someone suggested that he place the chili atop, the chili dog was created."

▼

Short-order cook Lionel Sternberger of Pasadena is believed to have invented the cheeseburger in the early 1920s in a small cafe on Colorado Boulevard. Although rival claims have been heard from Denver and Louisville, Ky., American Heritage magazine gave Pasadena the nod.

▼

An orange drink invented in L.A. in 1926 is said to have acquired its name because customers would often say to owner Julius Freed, "Give me an orange, Julius."

miscelLAny

Tray mats at McDonald's made this claim: "It is estimated that one out of every 15 Southern Californians start his or her working career at McDonald's."

Tommy's Original World Famous Hamburgers, which opened its first stand half a century ago on Beverly Boulevard, has spawned many imitators (Tammy, Tonnie, Tommie, etc.). So many that founder Tommy Koulax successfully pursued more than 20 lawsuits to protect the eatery's name, according to the L.A. Business Journal.

Leftovers: Other gastronomic firsts claimed by L.A. include the chili size or chili burger (Tommy De Forest of Ptomaine Tommy's), the Moscow Mule drink (Cock 'n' Bull restaurant), and chiffon cake (Harry Baker, a Hollywood insurance salesman).

i'll be your waiter and my name is none of your business

Pondering the menu in a West L.A. deli, Toni Sparano idly asked the waitress whether she should have the home fries or the tomatoes with her scrambled eggs.

Snapped the waitress: "I can't manage your life for you."

▼

A diner at a snooty French restaurant in San Pedro complained to the waiter that the lettuce in his salad was brown and wilted.

The waiter responded: "Would you like more dressing?"

Another diner complained that her cheese hors d'oeuvre contained no cheese.

"You ate it," the waiter countered.

▼

At Musso and Frank, the Hollywood landmark, diners seem to take a perverse delight in the occasional gruffness of the waiters.

Dean Hansell of L.A recalled the time a waiter brought him a Caesar salad and asked if he wanted fresh pepper.

"I replied, 'Yes,'" said Hansell, "whereupon he grabbed the pepper shaker on my table and proceeded to shake pepper on my salad."

Robert Light of Sherman Oaks once asked a passing waiter for the correct time.

The waiter's response: "That's not my table."

the great french dip debate

Two different L.A. eateries—both of them founded just after the turn of the century—claim to have invented the French dip sandwich.

Philippe's said it happened in 1918 when a customer's roll was dropped accidentally into a roasting pan at the downtown cafe. The customer, a policeman named Frenchy, ate it anyway—and liked it so much that he returned the next day and asked that his roll be dunked again. Soon, the dish caught on.

Not so, said Cole's, also a downtown favorite. According to bartender Jimmy Barela, a Cole's chef created the sandwich years earlier than Philippe's claim—and by request. Recalled Barela: "A fellow asked, 'Can you dip that bun into the juice?' He said, 'They (the buns) are too hard. They hurt my gums.' Pretty soon someone else said, 'Can you make me one of those?'"

An idea whose time had not come: In the early 1980s, the J.R. Grace Restaurant Co. placed American and Chinese restaurants side by side. Their names: Reuben's and Woo-Ben's. Woo-Ben's soon failed.

After auto crashed through a window, this Beverly Hills restaurant wanted to avoid a repeat experience.

We like sushi, but...

more evidence that l.a. is a cultural melting pot

Corned beef tacos on St. Patrick's Day at the Que Pasa restaurant, Sherman Oaks.

▼

Teriyaki tacos, with American cheese optional, at S.K. Restaurant and Coffee Shop, midtown L.A.

▼

Kosher pizza at Kosher Nostra, mid-town L.A.

▼

Fortune cookies with messages in English and Spanish at City Wok restaurant, Toluca Lake.

▼

Grape-and-brie quesadillas at Trump's, West Hollywood.

▼

Free sushi on Wednesdays at Timmy Nolan's, a Toluca Lake restaurant priding itself on being "In the Irish-California Tradition."

▼

Avocado cha-shu tacos (American cheese, barbe-cued pork, avocado, lettuce and tomato on corn tortillas) at Magu's Famous Burgers, Culver City.

▼

Hot dogs, doughnuts and Indian dishes at Tandoor Indian Food & Stan's Donuts, Westwood.

▼

German spaghetti at the Curry House, a Japanese restaurant, Little Tokyo.

Some surviving pioneer restaurants of L.A.:

Cole's, downtown, 1908

Philippe's, downtown, 1908

Musso and Frank, Hollywood, 1919

Pacific Dining Car, west of downtown, 1921

Tam O'Shanter, Los Feliz, 1922

Original Pantry, downtown, 1924

La Golondrina, Olvera Street, 1924

Les Freres Taix, Echo Park, 1927

El Cholo, mid-town, 1927

El Coyote, Park La Brea, 1931

Canter's, Fairfax, 1931

Little Joe's, Chinatown, 1932

Clifton's Cafeteria, downtown (Broadway), 1935

Lawry's, La Cienega Boulevard, 1938

Du-par's, Farmer's Market, 1938

A Hollywood landmark, circa 1928.

99¢

made
with recycled
newspapers

BURGER KING®
IS COMMITTED TO
BEING THE BEST!

A napkin that seems to promise
burgers with lots of fiber.

The apple of their eye?

Sink Your Teeth Into the
"Best" Buger in Santa Barbara

No thanks.

```
JACK IN THE  BOX
   10/11/94   7:53 AM  06#1
     ORDER  #97

1  SOURDH BRKFT        1.99

        SUBTOTAL       1.99
             TAX       0.16
        D-THRU         2.15


TRY OUR NEW CHICKEN CAESAR
WE HAVE A SECURITY GUARD!!!
```

For customers who need help
when they tangle with the
Chicken Caesar.

TASTY FOOD
GOOD SERVICE
LOW PRICES
LUNCH.DINNER

DIE IN OR TO-GO

OPEN 7 DAYS A WEEK
MON. - SAT. 10:30 AM - 9:00 PM
SUN   11:00 AM - 9:00 PM

For the truly adventurous
in dining.

S-K-A INTERESTS

RENT TO OWN

99¢ CHINESE FOOD

Can you really have your
take-out and rent it too?

One Coupon Per Table · Good for up to 403 guests at one
table Not valid with any other coupon or offer

There's always a catch to
these offers.

movie dialog that only an angeleno could love

"As bad as there is in L.A…and that's as bad as there is."
Paul Newman in "Harper," after client asks how "bad" are the people mixed up with her husband.

"Middle of a drought and the water commissioner drowns. Only in L.A."
Jack Nicholson in "Chinatown."

"A city where the only cultural advantage is that you can make a right turn on a red light." **Woody Allen in "Annie Hall."**

"This is KTTV studios in Hollywood, to Mt. Wilson. We are being attacked by the Slime People." **Robert Hutton in "The Slime People."**

"People turning south on the freeway were startled to see three flying saucers, high over Hollywood Boulevard." **Narrator in "Plan 9 From Outer Space."**

"It was one of those California Spanish houses everyone was nuts about. This one must have cost somebody about thirty thousand bucks."
Fred MacMurray, describing L.A. mansion in "Double Indemnity."

"Who needs a car in Los Angeles? We've got the best public transportation system in the world."
Bob Hoskins in "Who Framed Roger Rabbit" (the film was set in the '40s).

"I'm Italian. But I was born in Tarzana." **Danny DeVito in "Get Shorty."**

"I thought they were just some lucky (expletive) from Reseda."
Private eye Andrew Dice Clay's opinion of heavy metal band in "The Adventures of Ford Fairlane."

"If you had Brain One in that huge melon on top of your neck, you'd be living the sweet life out in Southern California's beautiful San Fernando Valley."

Bill Murray to fiendish spirit he encounters on streets of Manhattan, in "Ghostbusters II."

Private eye Jake Gittes (Jack Nicholson) to a water official: "Where are those orchards?" Official: "I said the northwest Valley." Gittes: "That's like saying they're in Arizona." **From the film "Chinatown."**

"Last year, somebody talked me into buying a ranch in the Valley."

Producer explaining why he's too broke to loan money to screenwriter Joe Gillis (William Holden) in "Sunset Boulevard."

"We're going to have a low coming in over Pa Sad Na — sorry, that's Pasadena." **Inept weathercaster Steve Martin in "L.A. Story."**

"Call Victorville and tell them we want the fastest plane they've got."

Desperate Army commander during flying saucer invasion in "The War of the Worlds."

"I'm the assistant manager of Food World in Burbank."

John Denver, describing his credentials to be God's messenger in "Oh God."

"I need road service for, uh, I don't know, let's say Inglewood."

Kevin Kline just before a confrontation with gang members in "Grand Canyon."

"The target for the A-bomb is the nest of Martian machines in the Puente hills." **TV announcer in "War of the Worlds."**

Film crew shooting cops and robbers scene with City Hall in background, circa 1930.

showbiz

When **film and TV predict the future**…Actors who are advertisements for themselves…My tomatoes look like Mickey Mouse…**Games that animators play** (was Jessica Rabbit really topless?)…In old Hollywood.

No sooner had Jack Nicholson been named host of the 1994 L.A. Police-Celebrity Golf Tournament than he was accused of wielding his club out of bounds — at a stop light in North Hollywood. A motorist claimed that Nicholson used the club to batter his car. The actor apparently thought he had been cut off. Nicholson hosted the golf tournament anyway, and got off this line at a film industry affair in his honor: "I'm touched and I'm fortunate. And I'm lucky to be at large."

▼

Can you tell us the color of his eyes? During the Woody Allen-Mia Farrow case, Farrow testified that a former husband of hers had offered to break Allen's legs. But the court blocked her from revealing which ex-spouse it was: former L.A. Philharmonic conductor Andre Previn or singer Frank Sinatra.

▼

Animal owners and others regularly send photos of purported Mickey Mouse images to Disneyland. A sampling: Dalmatian dog in L.A. with spots resembling Mickey's head, cat in Montebello with Mickey markings, shrubbery in Lompoc shaped like Mickey, Michigan baby's bottom with a Mickey birthmark, and tomato in Canoga Park resembling Mickey's head.

In this town, you need a name: The pop star who used to call himself Prince was refused a star on the Hollywood Walk of Fame. Part of the problem seemed to be the symbol that he now uses in place of a name. A Chamber of Commerce spokeswoman confirmed that his lack of a conventional name "was discussed," but would not elaborate.

▼

The film "Scenes From a Mall," which is set in the Beverly Center, was actually filmed at the Stamford, Connecticut, Town Center. Well, most of it. One bit in "Scenes" had to be shot elsewhere because the Connecticut mall didn't have a sushi bar.

▼

Say goodnight, Mick: Never let it be said the city of Pasadena can't get no satisfaction. When the Rolling Stones violated the city's midnight curfew at the Rose Bowl one night by three minutes, they were billed $6,000 in penalties. Yep, $2,000 a minute.

Elm Productions built an exact replica of Rodeo Drive in Mexico City, where it shot "The Taking of Beverly Hills." Scenes of the business center figured prominently in the film, but "we could hardly ask the city to close down the streets," said a spokesman.

▼

A production company won a $1.8 million judgment against a former employee accused of stealing the concept for a television game show. Name of the stolen show: "Anything for Money."

▼

The Country Walk of Fame in North Hollywood is the shortest such attraction on record. Because of a dispute with the city, the 16-year-old sidewalk exhibit has been confined to one star, Eddie Rabbit.

Any particular major? A trade paper advertised a stage laborer job, requiring the "ability to perform heavy physical labor." The ad concluded: "Bachelor's degree required."

▼

Movie production companies in L.A. whose names say it all: Roadkill Films, Rice & Beans Productions, The Anemic Co., Day Job Films, Dog & Pony Productions, Engulf & Devour Films, Pet Fly Productions.

Aspiring actor Dennis Woodruff covered his car with photos of himself.

Can she do both at the same time?

these movie folk advertise themselves

Would-be actors and others will try just about anything to get the attention of the film industry:

• Joe Brewster, an engineer for a Tucson TV station, ran a classified ad in the L.A. Times offering to trade 160 acres of Arizona land for a "good speaking role" in a movie. Responses included calls from "a guy who says he used to be pals with Howard Hughes" and another who "supposedly has lunch with (movie mogul) Jon Peters from time to time."

• Visitors to MCA's CityWalk saw a plane overhead with a banner proclaiming: **"World's funniest movie script. Need Producer."** A phone number followed.

• A license plate spotted in Santa Monica said: **OCASTME**.

• Message on a Jeep whizzing along the Santa Monica Freeway: **"I Brake for Auditions."**

• A woman outside 20th Century Fox Studios in West L.A. wore a sandwich board that said: **"Writer: Will Work for a Deal."**

Steve Mozena bought bus bench ad to promote himself.

201

games animators play

The creative folks who make animated films for children delight in slipping inside jokes and other pranks into their scenes:

- In Disney's "Beauty and the Beast" a barely noticeable frame shows crazy old Maurice coming upon a directional sign for the villages of Newhall, Valencia and Anaheim.

- When the evil Scar asks a prisoner to sing for him in "Lion King," the inmate breaks into the well-worn Disneyland anthem, "It's a Small World." Scar cuts him off, growling: "No, no, anything but that."

- Careful viewers of the laser disc version of "Who Framed Roger Rabbit," a Disney co-production, insisted they saw a pantyless Jessica Rabbit in one scene and a bare-breasted Jessica in another. Also spotted: graffiti on a phone booth reading, "For a good time, call Allison Wonderland." The phone number was Disney's.

- In the same movie, Roger Rabbit visits a friend in a hospital and is mistakenly rushed into surgery. Tied to a gurney, Roger screams as he flashes through doors labeled "Pathology," "Neurology," "Proctology" and so on. The last door on his terrifying journey is marked: "Burbank."

read your ticket carefully

The venerable theater at 6230 Sunset Boulevard has used many aliases since first opening in 1938:

- Earl Carroll's Vanities (1938-53)
- Moulin Rouge (1953-65)
- Hullabaloo (1965-68)
- Kaleidoscope (1968-69)
- Aquarius Theater (1969-93)
- Chevy Chase Theater (1993)
- Sunset Theater (1993-)

Anything but that! A newspaper listing summarized the film "Cleopatra" this way: "Queen of Egypt seduces Caesar, sees Mark Antony, asps herself."

A sign at the Pantages Theatre box office read:

BOX OFFICE HOURS

MONDAY
CLOSED

TUESDAY THRU SATURDAY
CLOSED

SUNDAY
CLOSED

hollywood predicts the future

Twenty-three years before Rodney King was beaten by cops in the Foothill Division, "Dragnet" aired an episode in which two African-Americans complained of police brutality after being pulled over by L.A. cops. Yes, they were from the Foothill Division.

▼

Dan Rowan and Dick Martin, stars of TV's "Laugh In," made outlandish predictions in a routine called "News of the Future." One of their sketches in the 1960s drew disbelieving laughter from the studio audience: they reported that it was 1988 and "President Reagan" was serving his second term. Reagan was governor of California at the time.

▼

In a 1949 episode of the old Burns and Allen radio show, the couple orders a cake with 100 candles. "Happy birthday, sir," the clerk says to George. In another episode, everyone laughs at George's neighbor, Harry Morton, because of his crackpot scheme to develop a new product — frozen yogurt.

▼

Several months before Metro Rail construction caused a section of Hollywood Boulevard to collapse, the movie "Speed" was released with a scene in which an out-of-control Red Line car explodes out of Hollywood Boulevard, leaving a gaping hole.

▼

Only months before the sudden fall of the communist government in the Soviet Union, the Fox Theater in Venice was playing this twin bill:

RUSSIA HOUSE

EVE OF DESTRUCTION

Are we passing judgment? A movie theater in Alhambra seemed to be drawing its own conclusions with this marquee listing of current attractions:

HOFFA
USED PEOPLE

miscelLAny

In the biography "Golden Boy," author Bob Thomas writes that as a teenager, actor William Holden used to delight in walking on his hands along the outer railing of Pasadena's Colorado Street bridge, also known as the Suicide Bridge.

Ex-Malibu resident Harry Reems, the porno star of "Deep Throat," renounced the movie business and moved to Park City, Utah, where he became a real estate agent.

harrumph for hollywood

"Strip the phony tinsel off Hollywood and you'll find the real tinsel underneath." — **Humorist and musician Oscar Levant.**

▼

"The only 'ism Hollywood believes in is plagiarism." — **Dorothy Parker.**

▼

"You could take all of the sincerity in Hollywood, put it in a flea's bellybutton and you'd still have room for four caraway seeds and an agent's heart." — **Comic Fred Allen.**

spelchek

A star on the Hollywood Walk of Fame honoring one Maurice Diller was removed after it was discovered that no film luminary bore that name. The space was then given to Mauritz Stiller, an early 20th-Century Swedish director for whom the honor was intended all along.

casting calls

"Females, 18-35, wtd to step on bugs with barefeet for short films, lrg feet welcome. Jeff at Squish Productions."

▼

"Seeking: Magician or hand model: To play 'Thing,' the disembodied hand that serves the Addams Family. Must be male Caucasian. Hand must be big, arms long and preferably double-jointed."

mr. malaprop

Studio boss Sam Goldwyn was famous for his assaults on the English language, including these gems:

- "Anyone who goes to a psychiatrist ought to have his head examined."
- "I read part of it all the way through."
- "A verbal contract isn't worth the paper it's written on."
- "Directors are always biting the hand that lays the golden egg."

Which one is the typographical error?

cinema verité, sort of

The makers of the "Columbo" TV show transformed a vacant store on Wilshire Boulevard into a make-believe jewelry shop, complete with a stylish nameplate. After the first day of shooting, they left their fake jewels in the front window. That night, the jewels were stolen — by real burglars.

▼

A film crew shooting a TV pilot on Terminal Island had to accept a citation from a county health inspector who stopped by to investigate the food at The Standing Eight cafe — not a real diner, but a set for the movie. What caught the inspector's eye was some 4-day-old chili and doughnuts used as props in an earlier scene. The film's location manager theorized that the county had been tipped off by prankish fishermen upset over the crew's presence.

▼

Kevin Brownlow, author of "Hollywood, The Pioneers," attributes this story to the late Hal Roach: The script for the 1929 movie, "Big Business," called for comics Laurel and Hardy to get into a fight that culminated with the total destruction of a man's home. The studio had already contracted with a couple on Dunleer Drive in West L.A. who agreed to have their house knocked down. But the film crew shot the scene at the wrong house — whose owners returned home

Politically correct listing?
Space was cramped on the movie marquee advertising the film, "Mrs. Parker and the Vicious Circle." So a portion of the title was abbreviated as follows: "Ms. Parker."

The expression "Little old lady from Pasadena" is believed to have originated on comedian Jack Benny's radio program.

The blinking red light atop the Capitol Records Tower spells out "HOLLYWOOD" in Morse Code.

Before the 1995 Academy Awards show, the publicist for Robert De Niro sent out this terse memo, explaining how to spell the actor's name.

just in time to see their place being destroyed by Stan and Ollie.

▼

When a car hit a pedestrian on the South Pasadena street where the TV show "Homefront" was being shot, actor Jonathan Terry ran to help. Terry, trained as a nurse, "started to perform a 'neuro check' by moving his finger from side to side and up and down, having the man follow his finger with his eyes," said a spokesman for the show. But Terry momentarily forgot he was dressed for his role as a Roman Catholic priest. "The poor man thought Jonathan was a priest performing last rites," said the spokesman. After explanations all around, the relieved pedestrian was found to have no serious injuries.

▼

The uniformed cop was chasing the purse-snatcher down Olvera Street when a passerby threw a crushing block on the culprit, sending him and the purse to the ground. Happy ending? Not quite. What the Good Samaritan didn't realize was that the officer and bad guy were actors, filming a scene for a new cop series. The actor/purse-snatcher was treated for minor injuries at a hospital. "The guy really gave him a good shoulder," marveled director Burt Armus.

Subject: spelling/typography of Robert De Niro's name

The correct spelling and typography of Robert De Niro's name is as follows:

De Niro, DE NIRO, or De Niro, is correct.

The "e" in "De" is _always_ the same size and case as the "iro" in "Niro".

Despite the way it has appeared elsewhere, it is _never_ De NIRO, or DE Niro.

There is _always_ a half space between "De" and "Niro."

old hollywood

L.A.'s first motion picture studio in the early 1900s was either (1) a defunct Chinese laundry on Olive Street where "The Heart of a Racing Tout" was shot or (2) an old mansion at 8th and Olive Streets where "In the Sultan's Power" was made. While film historians don't agree on which was first, there is agreement on what happened next: both locations became parking lots.

▼

D.W. Griffith's classic film "Birth of a Nation" premiered in L.A. in 1915 at Clune's Theater at 5th and Olive Streets. It was such an expensive production ($100,000) that local moviegoers were asked for the first time to fork over $2 for a ticket.

▼

In his biography of movie mogul Harry Cohn, author Bob Thomas notes that the list of words banned from movies in the 1930s included: cripes, Gawd, goose, hold your hat, in your hat, hell or damn (in most instances), SOB, tart and whore. Of course, there was also a ban against the f-word: fanny.

A chance to be near Marilyn Monroe for eternity.

▼

Charlie Chaplin's "City Lights" premiered at the grand opening of the Los Angeles Theater on Broadway in 1931. Chaplin's personal guests were Professor and Mrs. Albert Einstein.

▼

In 1937, miffed that it produced more than half the nation's movies but Hollywood got most of the credit, Culver City decided to rechristen itself Hollywood. It began a petition drive to accomplish the name change, arguing that since Hollywood was not an incorporated city, it had no legal right to the name. But the attempt failed. "In the end, Culver City was outflanked by the power of the outraged Hollywood stars," writer Leonard Leader recalled years later.

on location...

L.A.-area high schools have provided the setting for numerous movies and TV shows over the years. Some credits:

Whittier High: "Back to the Future," "Back to the Future 2"

Van Nuys High: "Fast Times at Ridgemont High"

Los Angeles High: The "Andy Hardy" movies, "Room 222"

Garfield High (East L.A.): "Stand and Deliver"

Beverly Hills High: "It's a Wonderful Life," "It Happened One Christmas," "The Bachelor and the Bobby Soxer"

Hughes Junior High (Woodland Hills): "Beethoven," "Karate Kid"

Excelsior High (Norwalk): "Grease 2"

Grant High (Van Nuys): "Clueless," "Casualty of Love"

Le Conte Junior High (North Hollywood): "Bye, Bye Birdie," "The Wonder Years," "Torch Song Trilogy"

Santa Monica High: "Rebel Without a Cause"

John Burroughs Junior High (Hancock Park): "Teen Wolf"

Torrance High: "Beverly Hills 90210"

San Pedro High: "My So-Called Life"

Hamilton High: "Mr. Novak," "The Trouble With Father," "Parker Lewis Can't Lose," "High School Confidential"

Venice High: "Grease"

Marshall High: "Rebel Without a Cause," "Grease"

Hollywood High: "Hollywood High"

Downtown L.A. traffic is a real challenge in "Blade Runner."

Some notable film and T.V. locations around the Southland:

City Hall: The Vatican in "The Thornbirds," U.S. Capitol in "The Jimmy Hoffa Story," Texas office of Lyndon Johnson in "LBJ," police headquarters in "Dragnet" series, and Daily Planet newspaper in "Superman" series.

Shrine Auditorium: Scene in which the star of "King Kong" breaks loose from his chains was filmed on its stage.

Union Station, North Alameda Street: Police station in "Blade Runner," played itself in "Union Station."

Bradbury Building, South Broadway: Gumshoe Wayne Rogers had his office there in "City of Angels." Androids ran loose in "Blade Runner."

Bonaventure Hotel, South Figueroa Street: Clint Eastwood foiled a would-be presidential assassin in "In the Line of Fire."

Sherman Oaks Galleria: One of the settings in "Fast Times at Ridgemont High."

An airport hangar at Van Nuys Airport: Closing scene in movie "Casablanca," in which Rick (Humphrey Bogart) bids farewell to Ilsa (Ingrid Bergman).

The University of Southern California: It has played the part of many rival schools, including: University of Alabama ("Forrest Gump"), UC Berkeley ("The Graduate"), UCLA ("Big Man on Campus") and Harvard ("Paper Chase"). USC also provided bell tower for Charles Laughton classic, "The Hunchback of Notre Dame."

Goat Butte Rocks: Volcanic outcropping above Malibu Creek was seen at the start of each "MASH" TV show.

United Methodist Church, La Verne: Where Dustin Hoffman pounded on church door to thwart wedding of his beloved to another in "The Graduate."

Bronson Caves, Griffith Park: Underground lair of TV's Batman.

Steps in 900 block of Vendome Street, Silver Lake: Comedy duo of Laurel and Hardy tried to ascend them while pushing a piano in "The Music Box," Academy Award-winning film of 1932.

Loyola University football field: Setting for action scenes in 1941 film, "Knute Rockne, All American." Film is best remembered for "Win One for the Gipper" speech made by an actor who received third billing — Ronald Reagan.

Passerby mimics sculptor Terry Allen's unusual work entitled "Corporate Head."

the arts

The naked lady of Malibu and other art wars…Dramatic moments that weren't in the program…**Literary figures** who were among us…The car wash as cultural monument…**Museums** that may not have been included in your guide book.

For a while, it looked like a Studio City car wash might be declared a cultural monument. Commissioners of the L.A. Cultural Heritage Board actually motored there to inspect its distinctive 55-foot-tall boomerang-shaped girders. After deliberating, the board said no, clearing the way for a developer to demolish the facility but disappointing its fans. "It's not a cultural monument," agreed television actor William Griffis. "But it certainly is a handy place to get your car washed."

▼

For years, the body of a failed train-robber named Elmer McCurdy had been displayed as a mummy in Wild West shows. Then it was sent to a Long Beach amusement park, where it was billed as a wax dummy and hung from a gallows to thrill onlookers. Nobody realized it was an actual body until a technician accidentally pulled off one of Elmer's arms during the filming of a TV show in 1976. The remains were eventually buried in an Oklahoma cemetery.

▼

Most disillusioning disclaimer of the year: A theater group's program proclaimed, "The stereotypes portrayed in 'Winnie the Pooh' are in no way condoned by the Young Artists Ensemble, and we have left them intact to preserve the author's original message. All bears do not like honey, not all donkeys are slow, not all piglets are easily frightened, and not all boys think that Winnie the Pooh can talk to them."

miscelLAny

Billionaire J. Paul Getty, who died in England in 1976, never visited the J. Paul Getty Museum, which opened in Pacific Palisades in 1974.

When John Marshall's "Monument of the Unknown Government Employee" went on display in City Hall, government employees grumbled. The art work depicted, among other things, a man with a briefcase and a coffee pot on a pedestal. City workers took one look at the coffee pot and figured it was a slam at them for taking too many breaks. Not so, declared a surprised Marshall, who said the piece was merely intended to make workers re-examine their roles.

definitely not on the program

When the applause died down after a solo by trumpeter Ashley Williams, several people at a Pasadena music festival ran for the exits. "The bandstand was situated next to a parking structure, three or four stories high," explained a spokes-woman. "When Ashley hit a high note, about 10 to 20 car alarms went off."

▼

When a forgetful concertmaster began a Hollywood Bowl performance without the custom-ary singing of the "Star-Spangled Banner," the audi-ence was visibly disturbed. Before long, people were rising from their seats and spontaneously singing the national anthem. The mini-revolt had a happy ending when the concertmaster realized his mistake and directed the orchestra to join in.

▼

A synopsis of the play "Two & Two Makes Sex" said that when George has an affair with a younger woman, his wife plots revenge with "unpredictable" results. And so it was on opening night at the La Mirada Theater: actor Ric Watson in the role of George broke his leg during a scene in which he was supposed to jog through a door. He hopped off the stage on one leg, the curtain came down, and an ambulance was summoned. Mused producer Yolanda Robinson: "We said, 'Break a leg,' and 30 minutes later he did."

literary figures among us

Upton Sinclair, the Pulitzer Prize-winning author, moved to Monrovia in the 1940s after Pasadena became too congested for him. The Sinclair house is at 464 N. Myrtle Ave.

▼

F. Scott Fitzgerald spent his last years in an apartment at 1403 N. Laurel Avenue in West Hollywood. "To economize we shared the same maid," wrote Sheilah Graham, his lover and neighbor. Fitzgerald was 44 when he died of a heart attack in 1940, in Graham's apartment a few blocks away on North Hayworth Avenue.

▼

William Faulkner, during his stormy stay as a screenwriter for Columbia Studios, lived on Whitley Terrace above Hollywood. One day, Faulkner is said to have announced that he was leaving early "to work at home." He couldn't be found for days. Only later did the studio learn that by "home," Faulkner meant Oxford, Miss.

Fitzgerald

▼

Theodore Dreiser ("An American Tragedy") lived in flats on Alvarado Street and Sunset Boulevard, but didn't produce his best work in L.A.

▼

James Jones wrote the last chapter of "From Here to Eternity," set in Hawaii at the time of the Pearl Harbor attack, in a North Hollywood trailer park on Lankershim Boulevard.

Faulkner

▼

Nathanael West wrote "The Day of the Locust" after spending a hot and unpleasant summer during the Depression at a boardinghouse on Ivar Avenue in Hollywood. "Another name for Ivar Street was Lysol Alley," he wrote.

where else can you find art like this?

A kinetic sculpture at the L.A. Museum of Neon Art commemorated one of baseball's strangest moments—when a motorized tarpaulin machine ran over St. Louis outfielder Vince Coleman and broke his leg. The sculpture's tiny tarp rolled across a baseball diamond under miniature stadium lights toward its inevitable destination while an instrumental version of "Take Me Out to the Ball Game" played and a voice cried, "Watch out, Vince!" The artist: Dave Quick.

▼

After workers salvaged a 116-ton rock that was about to fall onto Pacific Coast Highway in Malibu, sculptor Brett-Livingston Strong used huge chunks of it to fashion a likeness of John Wayne. The sculpture sold for a reported $1 million.

Sculptor Steve Simon constructed a 2,000-foot-long blood vessel to call attention to the American Red Cross' needs. Five hundred fluorescent tubes were covered by a red fabric, then lit up at night. Simon also glued together 35,000 discarded cigarette packs to create an 11-foot-long filter tip, which the American Lung Assn. exhibited in its "Kiss Your Butt Goodby" campaign.

▼

Some people are content to seek out the autographs of celebrities. John Pate, a standup comic, went after their tread marks, too. Pate's contributors let him splash watercolors on their tire treads, then drove over canvases spread on the pavement. "The idea came to me while I was in a museum looking at some pop art. I figured you could run a car across a canvas and get the same effect," said Pate. His autographed collection included treads by boxer Ray (Boom Boom) Mancini, comic Phyllis Diller and actor Ed Marinaro.

▼

Yukinori Yanagi's organic art work at L.A. Contemporary Exhibitions was entitled "World Flag Ant Farm Project." Yanagi created various flags of the world with colored grains of sand, then invited his ants to remove or rearrange the grains.

The goal: to eventually dissolve the flags and let the work evolve "into one universal flag."

▼

Her intention, guerrilla pianist Sandra Tsing Loh said, was to bring land and sea life into "symphonic harmony with nature's eternal rhythm." That's why Loh, backed by the Topanga Symphony Orchestra, pounded out her composition, "Night of the Grunion," one night on a piano set up at Malibu's Surfrider Beach. About 600 spectators listened to the music and watched the grunion come ashore. The same Loh once serenaded rush-hour drivers from a parking structure near the Harbor Freeway.

▼

Smog art at a UC Riverside exhibition included 17 corked bottles containing pieces of gauze that had been exposed to polluted air. "You can remove the cork from a bottle and smell something really nauseous," guaranteed a museum spokesman.

▼

An art exhibit illustrating headaches was presented at the Santa Monica Public Library. Artists who contributed paintings, photographs and prints to the show said they drew on their own personal suffering for inspiration.

Wall at Museum of Contemporary Art on Bunker Hill was patterned after outline of Marilyn Monroe's body in a famous pinup photo. Museum designer Arata Isozaki, an ardent fan of the actress, dubbed it "the Monroe Curve."

murder and mayhem from los feliz to malibu:

L.A. has been the setting for many mystery novels. You can find private eyes and flatfoots stalking through:

- **Los Feliz:** "Double Indemnity," by James Cain.
- **East L.A.:** "Zoot Suit Murders," by Thomas Sanchez.
- **South-Central:** "Devil in a Blue Dress," by Walter Mosley.
- **MacArthur Park:** "The Choirboys," by Joseph Wambaugh.
- **Venice:** "The Big Fix," by Roger Simon.
- **Little Tokyo:** "Rising Sun," by Michael Crichton.
- **Laurel Canyon:** "The Long Goodbye," by Raymond Chandler.
- **Santa Monica:** "North of Montana," by April Smith.
- **Malibu:** "Voodoo Ltd.," by Ross Thomas.

"Back Seat Dodge '38," an assemblage by Edward Kienholz, was a lusty, beer-bottle-festooned scene of a couple making whoopee in a car. Some politicians tried to ban the work after its debut at the County Museum of Art.

the art wars

The neighbors were mortified when a Saudi sheik painted the flesh, hair and body parts on four Greek statues in front of his Beverly Hills mansion. He eventually moved away and the estate was leveled after a 1980 fire.

▼

A David Hockney painting at the bottom of the Hollywood Roosevelt swimming pool was deemed a hazard by local authorities, concerned that it might hinder a lifeguard's view. The state Legislature settled the dispute by passing a bill declaring the painting to be safe. Hockney used brushes on cutoff broomsticks to create the art work, which resembles a school of swimming parentheses.

The city of Rancho Palos Verdes seemed ready to plow under a 37-foot-tall earthen sculpture of a nude woman sunbathing above Hawthorne Boulevard. But after tests showed the curvaceous mound was stable, it was allowed to remain. Owner Ted Gardner said he commissioned the sculpture for the amusement of passing motorists.

▼

For Mardis Gras, the Orleans restaurant in West L.A. trotted out life-sized cutouts of three bare-breasted women and placed them on an exterior balcony. When some neighbors demanded that they be covered up, the artist who created the figures retorted: "There are probably people out there who would say of the Venus de Milo, 'What you've got here is a naked amputee.'"

▼

When a 60-foot-tall painting of a naked lady appeared above a tunnel on Malibu Canyon Road, spectators gathered by the hundreds to admire the acrobatic artistry of its creator, a Northridge artist who had hung from ropes to paint the dancing figure. But officialdom viewed the "Pink Lady of Malibu" as a trespasser on county property. Workers used spray guns to paint over the image.

Malibu's Pink Lady.

keeping the gods happy

A worker for the county Natural History Museum stopped at a gas station to buy cigarettes. Asked what brand she preferred, she said it didn't matter because she wasn't going to smoke them. Intrigued, the attendant asked what else the cigarettes could be used for. "Would you believe an offering to the gods?" the museum worker replied. She wasn't joking. In return for the loan of some sacred Indonesian heirlooms, museum officials had agreed to make a show of respect for the objects twice a week, in keeping with that nation's traditions. Approved offerings included the petals of five kinds of flowers—mixed with tobacco.

Jonathan Borofsky's "Ballerina Clown" is a landmark at
Rose and Main in Venice. But few took the sculpture seriously until Sunset magazine included the transvestite per-
former in an article on L.A.'s "world-class art." The blue
brassiere must have been the convincer.

cultural shrines of a different kind

The Banana Museum, Altadena. More than 15,000 banana-related artifacts, including a banana purse, banana umbrella, movie poster of "Herbie Goes Bananas" and a banana bearing a sequined image of Michael Jackson.

▼

World Wrestling Museum and Hall of Fame, Sun Valley. Memorabilia of such ring luminaries as Gorgeous George and The Fabulous Moolah.

▼

Museum of Jurassic Technology, Santa Monica. Has nothing to do with dinosaurs but does boast such exhibits as a horn that purportedly grew from a woman's head and a collection of extinct 19th century French moths.

▼

Bigfoot Museum, Venice. Exhibits include satellite photos of Martian rock formations resembling profile of Tammy Faye Bakker and jowls of Sen. Edward Kennedy.

▼

International Brassiere Museum at Frederick's of Hollywood. Garments that once adorned movie stars, including a Lana Turner slip, a Judy Garland nightgown and a dress worn by Milton Berle on his TV show.

▼

Sadly, no longer with us: **Foot and Toe Museum** (Long Beach), **Hopalong Cassidy Museum** (Downey), **Exotic Dancers Hall of Fame** (San Pedro) and **Weird Museum**, (Hollywood).

Kissing machine (circa 1939) at Max Factor Makeup Museum in Hollywood tested lipstick by pressing rubberized lips together under 10 pounds of tension. Factor thought that was the ideal kissing pressure.

Could this be L.A.'s first piece of drive-by art? Actually, Jonathan Borofsky's metal sculpture of four figures riddled with holes is entitled "Molecule Men." It can be found outside the Roybal Federal Center.

Buildings as art

The Capitol Records
building.

Cars arriving at the Chiat/Day ad agency in Venice pass through a giant inverted set of binoculars. Huge replicas of the Seven Dwarfs appear to be holding up an office building at Disney headquarters in Burbank. They are modern reminders of a time when buildings in L.A. resembled everything from animals, doughnuts and pieces of fruit to shoes, coffee cups and cameras.

It began with the arrival of the automobile in the 1920s. Merchants had to find ways to catch the eyes of passing motorists, and the oddly designed buildings at least did that.

A chain of giant chili bowls advertised: "We cook our beans backwards — you only get the hiccups." Restaurateur Herbert Somborn built the original Brown Derby on Wilshire Boulevard after supposedly bragging that he could sell food anywhere, even out of a very large hat.

Chiat/Day's binocular entrance.

Coffee shop on Wilshire Boulevard.

Over time, most of the eccentric structures became only memories. The Ugly Dog Cafe became Ugly Dog Records before being put to sleep. The huge green vegetable atop Pickle Bill's served as a Tiki war god at Kelbo's Barbecue, then disappeared.

Fortunately, there are some survivors. A portion of the Derby landed atop a Korean restaurant around the corner from its original site. The ship-shaped Coca-Cola bottling plant and Randy's Donuts remain. And the Hollywood headquarters of Capitol Records still resembles a stack of LPs.

The original Tail o' the Pup hot dog stand was faced with its biggest to-go order a few years ago when it lost its lease. But the 17-foot-long plaster frankfurter managed to find a new home in West Hollywood.

The Seven Dwarfs holding up Disney building

Auto salvage firm decorated its building with a 1933 Willys.

Even vehicles became works of art: John Goli and auto in the shape of a hiking boot, parked outside his West L.A. shoe repair shop.

Photo Credits

Restaurants
Page 186: Perry C. Riddle. p. 188: John Hayes. p. 191: Benjamin Reuben. p. 195: Gerald P. Jones.

Show Biz
Page 198: L.A. Public Library. p. 201: Jose Galvez (top left); Michael Sendlewski (top right). p. 205: David Rae Morris. p. 208-209: Warner Brothers.

The Arts
Page 210-217: L.A. Times. p. 218: Theodora Litsios. p. 219: Ken Lubas (bottom). p. 220: L.A. Times (top), J. Albert Diaz (bottom left), L.A. Public library (bottom right). p. 221: L.A. Times (all). p. 224: Bob Leavitt.

Acknowledgments
I'd like to thank the many readers and colleagues who have contributed to the column and are greatly responsible for any success it has achieved. Aside from those mentioned elsewhere in the book, I'm especially grateful to:

Jill Angel, Ken Ayeroff, Jim Bates, Jay Berman, Jeff Bliss, Tom Bratter, Ruth Breslow, Ron Burton, Mary Carver, Paul Cate, Joe Cislowski, Gil Chesterton, T.C. Cirillo, Douglas Clark, Betty Cockerill, Howard Cohen, Edward Conklin, Miles Corwin, Joyce Crawford, Jerry Cowle, Warren Davidson, Paul Dean, Cliff Dektar, Ski Demski, Mark Denis, Dick and Vanessa Deskin, Scott Dewees, Lynn Dickhoff, Bill Dougherty, Georgia Durgin, Jeff Earle, Joe Eisaman, Craig Endler, Art Fein, Walter Fluent, Everett Fong, Glady Foreman, Sterling Franklin, George French, Henk Friezer, Alan Frisbie, Victor Frisbie, Zsa Zsa Gershick, Pat Goldstein, Roger Hammond, Larry Harnisch, Lee Harris, Ron Harris, Roy Harris, Will Harriss, Steven Herbert, Nieson Himmel, Scott Hopkinson, Greg Horbachevsky, Lisa Jacobi, D. S.Jenkins, Brad Johnson, Richard Kales, Elizabeth Kates, Stan Kelton, Ronald Koegler, Carolyn Kozo, Tom LaBonge, Gary Leonard, Meyer Levine, Eric Lichtblau, Cyndy Lieberman, June Lockhart.

Also: Kate Mayer, Sara Meric,Tom Mills, Bennett Mintz, Marie Moog, Byron Myhre, T.K. Nagano, Greg Nelson, Paul Newman, Jay Olins, Mike Owen, Thomas Pleasure, Bob Pool, Cecilia Rasmussen, Val Rodriguez, Rick Rofman, Eric Rose, Steve Rosenberg, Gary Rosenblatt, Don Salper, Michael Saltzman, Ed Schlossman, Nick Scott, Susanne Shapiro, Joe Shea, Joyce Clark Shults, Stan Sieger, Rich Simon, Will Simpson, Barry Sloan, Bruce Smith, Rockey Spicer, Nick Stein, Dan Steinbrocker, Marian Tanaka, Jim Thornton, Luis Torres, Robert Torres, Bob Tur, Elyse Verse, Art Vinsel, Beth Wagner, Phyllis Waggner, Bob Welkos, John M. Wilson, Mae Woods, Barry Zepel and Elliot Zwiebach. And my apologies to contributors I have omitted.

I'd also like to thank the Times editors who helped mold the column through the years, including Pete King, Dick Barnes, Paul Lieberman, Cyndy Craft, Jim Bornemeier, Don Hunt, Rick Barrs and Sheila Daniel, as well as my bosses Carol Stogsdill and Leo Wolinsky.

In the preparation of this book, I'm enormously grateful to three indefatigable souls: Patricia Moritz, the designer; Don Michel, the Times' Syndicate director of book development; and, especially, the editor, Noel Greenwood.

Also, I owe a debt of gratitude to L.A. Times Syndicate staffers Marilyn Shigetani for helping tame the electronic gremlins, Odin della-Catena and Dave Allison for research, Cathryn Irvine for promotion, and Ray Recendez, Susan Gross and Dan Chodos for scanning.

I also want to thank Lacy Hamilton for her proofreading.

Finally, I'm grateful to my wife, Tia, and children, Sarah and James, for putting up with my absences and with my interest in strange people and events. And, oh yes, thanks Mom, Marie T. Harvey, without whom I wouldn't be here.